ACKNOWLEDGMENTS

Diving into the lives of some of history's most memorable people was a delight and a pleasure. Many thanks to my agent Claire (the Wise) Anderson-Wheeler, editor Julie (the Visionary) Matysik and Udayana Lugo, and Val Howlett, Frances J. Soo Ping Chow, Cisca L. Schreefel, and all at Running Press Kids.

Running Press Kids
Hachette Book Group
1290 Avenue of the Americas, New York, NY 10104
www.runningpress.com/rpkids
@RP_Kids

Printed in China

First Edition: September 2020

Published by Running Press Kids, an imprint of Perseus Books, LLC, a subsidiary of Hachette Book Group, Inc. The Running Press Kids name and logo is a trademark of the Hachette Book Group.

The Hachette Speakers Bureau provides a wide range of authors for speaking events. To find out more, go to www.hachettespeakersbureau.com or call (866) 376-6591.

The publisher is not responsible for websites (or their content) that are not owned by the publisher.

Print book cover and interior design by Frances J. Soo Ping Chow

Library of Congress Control Number: 2020930882

ISBNs: 978-0-7624-9661-7 (hardcover), 978-0-7624-9662-4 (ebook)

1010

10 9 8 7 6 5 4 3 2 1

FOR MY FATHER,

who gifted me my love of history

...

CONTENTS

INTRODUCTION

If you had to describe yourself in one word, what would it be? What sums up the *very* most important thing people should know about you? How would you like to be remembered? Choose thoughtfully. It may be a word that ends up being joined to your name *forever*.

In this book, you'll meet some of the most memorable people in history. Good, great, magnificent, and beloved people. Terrible, cruel, and bloodthirsty people. They were all leaders who made an impression that has lasted (some for thousands of years!).

First, consider the greats in the following pages. Each leader here is great in his or her own way. Some have fascinating legends attached to their births or to their lives. (Can the stars really predict when a great person will be born? You'll have to read to find out.) These leaders come from different places around the world at different periods in history. But there are some things they all have in common: They respected others; often they were big-picture thinkers; they were willing to listen to those they served; they learned from their mistakes; they thought about their actions in the long term, not just about what was beneficial at the moment. Sometimes the change they wanted wouldn't be achieved in their lifetimes, but they laid the groundwork so that things would be better for those who came after them. When times were tough, these great people rose to the challenges before them.

When you look at the so-called terribles in this book, you'll find that they also have some things in common. They usually put themselves first. They didn't have respect for anyone. Instead of learning and changing with the times or the circumstances, they were closed off to new ideas. Some of them would do *anything* to get what they wanted.

Remember, though, that humans are complicated. Some of the greats you'll find here did terrible things, too. Some of the terribles weren't *all* that bad. Sometimes a person is considered great by one group but terrible by another. There's a very well-known expression that you'll want to consider when you read about each of these greats and terribles: "History is written by the victor." That means that the story we remember about a person or an event may not be the whole story, just one side of it.

As you read this book, be sure to ask yourself: What qualities do you think make a leader great? Who are the greatest heroes in history (or even today), in your opinion? Would you rather have a leader who is powerful or one who is wise? Is it better to break with tradition, to follow it, or to adapt it to suit your circumstances?

And finally, ask yourself: How do you want people to remember you?

Signed,

Joanne the Curious

THE GREATS

HATSHEPSUT

THE GREAT ROYAL WIFE, EGYPT'S FEMALE PHARAOH

REIGN: 1479–1458 BCE

FATHER: Pharaoh Thutmose I / **MOTHER:** Queen Ahmose

SUCCESSOR: Thutmose III

OTHER NAMES: God's Wife, Lady of the Land to Its Limits, the Great One, the Foremost of Noble Ladies

• • •

WHAT WAS SO GREAT ABOUT HATSHEPSUT?

Hatshepsut (pronounced hat-SHEP-soot) wasn't the *only* female leader that Egypt ever had—several women before and after her served as regent for boys who were too young to rule. She also wasn't the only one with the title "Great Royal Wife." This was given to the chief wife of each pharaoh (pharaohs typically had many wives). But historians think Hatshepsut was the first Egyptian woman to declare herself pharaoh, the title used for those considered the supreme ruler of Egypt and descendant of the gods. That took some great courage! But it's also why she was nearly forgotten for thousands of years: archeologists who found carvings of her thought she was actually a man!

GREAT BEGINNINGS

Hatshepsut was the daughter of Pharaoh Thutmose I, and it's said that she was his favorite child. She married her half-brother Thutmose II to keep the royal bloodline going. When he died, though, the throne should have passed to Thutmose III, his son by a lesser wife. But since the boy was too young, Hatshepsut—his stepmother—became regent. It seems that Hatshepsut enjoyed ruling so much that, seven years later, she decided to promote herself to pharaoh.

THE BEARDED LADY

Most queens wear gowns and fancy jewelry to special court events. But not Hatshepsut. She wore a fake beard. Made from braided goat hair, the beard was positioned on the center of her chin and held in place by a cord that wrapped around her ears. It wasn't her personal fashion statement by any means. All the pharaohs wore them to symbolize their connection to the bearded Osiris, one of the most important Egyptian gods. In wearing the beard, Hatshepsut was saying, "Forget that I'm a woman. I'm just like every other pharaoh."

When she was regent, statues and carvings depicted Hatshepsut as a woman. But after she became pharaoh, she was usually depicted in men's clothing. She even had statues made of her daughter Nefurure wearing male clothing, probably because she hoped that she, too, would one day be pharaoh.

Hatshepsut wasn't the only woman leader in history who dressed as a man to earn her people's respect. Women throughout the centuries have led armies into battle while dressed as men. Joan of Arc is the most famous example, but there are many others. Hangaku, the twelfth-century daughter of a Japanese samurai, dressed as a man to help defend Takadachi Castle from attackers. Some women rulers dressed as men for other reasons. Cristina of Sweden—who was often called the "Girl King" or "The King of Sweden"—said men's clothes were just more comfortable to wear!

PARDON HER DUST

In Hatshepsut's time, nothing said "I'm powerful" like a bunch of building projects. You couldn't walk a block without finding something under construction during her reign: temples, shrines, or monuments. But pyramids were already *so* last millennium. Hatshepsut wanted something unique—the biggest, most amazing mortuary temple the world had ever seen. Hatshepsut's *Deir el-Bahri*—the first temple in what was later to become the Valley of the Kings—is still considered to be one of the finest ancient buildings in existence. It was built into the side of a giant cliff, commanding attention for miles around. The design features three stories of colonnades and terraces accessed by two long ramps. (In Hatshepsut's day, there were also elaborate gardens on each terrace. On the bottom floor, there were papyrus pools and frankincense trees from foreign lands.) Outside of the temple, she built matching obelisks, the tallest in the world at the time. In fact, the one that remains standing is *still* the tallest ancient obelisk in the world.

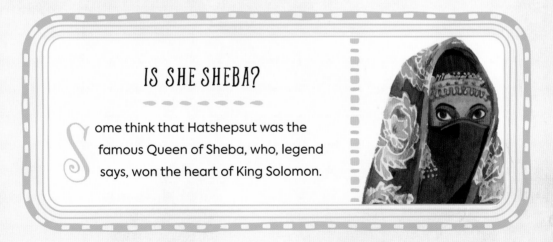

IS SHE SHEBA?

• • • • • •

Some think that Hatshepsut was the famous Queen of Sheba, who, legend says, won the heart of King Solomon.

HERE'S LOOKING AT ME

Hatshepsut wasn't exactly a humble ruler. For example, she told everyone that her father was actually the god Amun and that he wanted her to be pharaoh. "To look upon her was more beautiful than anything; her splendor and her form were divine," reads an inscription inside Deir el-Bahri. Historians think Hatshepsut dictated it herself. Also inside the temple are wall carvings telling of her amazing birth, as

THE MYSTERY OF
THE MUMMY'S TOOTH

T here was nothing very special about KV60, an out-of-the-way, dusty tomb in Hatshepsut's temple. When he opened it in 2006, Dr. Zahi Hawass—one of the world's foremost Egyptologists— found two female mummies inside: one in a coffin, one lying on the floor. There was no fancy sarcophagus like King Tut's, no worldly goods left to take into the underworld. Hawass had been looking everywhere for Hatshepsut's mummy, but it couldn't be one of these two. Surely the Great Royal Wife had received a better burial than this!

But Hawass also guessed that Hatshepsut's mummy might have been hidden to protect it from grave robbers, so he checked out the two abandoned mummies anyway. In the mouth of the one on the floor, he found a space for a missing tooth. This reminded him of something: a box with Hatshepsut's name on it, found in another tomb. The box contained a tooth that fit perfectly in the space in the mummy's mouth. Using DNA testing that took more than a year to complete, Hawass finally confirmed that the mummy was indeed Hatshepsut. She can now be seen at the Royal Mummy Rooms at the Egyptian Museum in Cairo, looking not as divine as she claimed while she was living, but looking pretty great for someone who's several thousand years old!

well as countless statues of her—Hatshepsut as a sphinx; Hatshepsut as a pharaoh; Hatshepsut as the child of a goddess. So many statues were made in her time that there's hardly a major museum in the world today that doesn't have a Hatshepsut statue in its collection. There's even a whole Hatshepsut Room at the Metropolitan Museum of Art in New York City.

Hatshepsut

But after Hatshepsut died, someone (possibly her stepson) decided to try to wipe out any trace of her reign as pharaoh. Inscriptions about her and pictures of her were chiseled out of walls. Obelisks and statues from her time were smashed. So much was destroyed that Egyptologists didn't really know much about her until the nineteenth century. And even though the giant temple of Deir el-Bahri was dedicated to her, archeologists didn't find her mummy until 2007 (see page 6).

 Hatshepsut's Legacy

Hatshepsut's greatest legacy is not her incredible temple, which still stands in Egypt today, but rather her belief that a woman could be just as good a leader as a man.

WHEN HATSHEPSUT WAS PHARAOH...

the chariot was the vehicle of choice in the civilized world

the legendary King Solomon was on the throne in nearby Judea

people in Shang dynasty China were making vessels (such as bowls) out of bronze

a volcano erupted on the Greek island of Santorini. Some say it caused the mythical city of Atlantis to disappear

CYRUS the GREAT

ANCIENT PERSIA'S MOST POWERFUL RULER

REIGN: circa 559–529 BCE

FATHER: Cambyses I / **MOTHER:** Mandane of Media
SUCCESSOR: Cambyses II

• • •

WHAT WAS SO GREAT ABOUT CYRUS?

Cyrus introduced a new idea to the world: that people didn't have to give up their own culture or beliefs in order to be part of a bigger empire. They could, instead, live harmoniously together under a single ruler. This was the first time in history that had ever happened.

BECOMING GREAT

There's a legend that Cyrus's grandfather believed he would be dethroned by his grandson, so he wanted to have him killed when he was a baby (see page 12). But Cyrus grew up to be a great military leader, raising armies and conquering kingdoms. If you look at today's map, his kingdom would take up all of the Middle East and parts of what's now Afghanistan. It was the custom that the conquering army took the spoils of those they defeated, such as jewelry, horses, statues, and, of course, land. The leaders of the losing kingdom were usually executed and the people were forced to adopt the religion of the conqueror.

But Cyrus did things differently. After he conquered a kingdom, he let the leader he'd defeated live and then gave him a job, such as governor or advisor. Cyrus directed his armies to give back the spoils that they'd taken. He let the

YOU'VE GOT MAIL

Think about the huge distances from one end of Cyrus's empire and the other. Even today, it would take the better part of a day to cross it in a jet plane. In Cyrus's day, it would take months. If there was an important message or news that had to get out to all of the empire, there wasn't a good way to make it happen. So Cyrus started connecting different roads in the empire into one called the Great Royal Road. It was about 1,500 miles long and wasn't completed until after Cyrus's death—in the time of a later Persian emperor, Darius the Great. During his rule, though, Cyrus developed what's considered to be the world's first postal system. Government messages would be sent out by horse riders and wagons. At post houses positioned along the route, riders waited with fresh horses. They would take the message to the next post house. There were around eighty post houses along the road. The horsemen were said to be very fast, and, like today's postal service, they delivered the mail no matter the weather.

conquered people continue to worship their own gods at their own temples. Cyrus even embraced parts of the cultures he ruled over. It's said he started wearing clothes like the people in some of his new kingdoms (in earlier days, *they* would have had to start dressing like him).

Cyrus's biggest conquest was Babylon, which had until then been the world's most powerful kingdom. The Babylonians had conquered the Jews and were holding

THE CYRUS CYLINDER

In 1879, while British archeologists were uncovering the ruins of Babylon, they found a small baked clay object that was less than a foot long. It had tiny cuneiform writing all over it.

When they began to translate the message, they found that it was a declaration from Cyrus, who had conquered the city. It became known as the Cyrus Cylinder.

In the message, Cyrus declared that he was now king, but having conquered this kingdom, he wanted peace. He said that the people of the kingdom were free to choose their own religion and didn't have to worship his gods. His government wouldn't look down on the Babylonians or insult them for their beliefs. He also said that he had let captive people go back to their own homelands and restore their temples there. He returned the spoils of war that were taken from the people by his army. He promised his government wouldn't take land without compensating the owner. He wouldn't allow any oppression to take place on his watch. If his administrators did oppress people, they would lose their jobs. Finally, he stated there would be no unpaid labor in his kingdom.

Some have called the Cyrus Cylinder the first declaration of human rights. It symbolizes tolerance, diversity, and freedom of religion. Today, the cylinder is on display at the British Museum in London, but there's also a replica of it at the United Nations in New York City.

Not everyone agrees about the significance of the Cyrus Cylinder. Some say its historical significance has been exaggerated. Others think the cylinder was just propaganda used during Cyrus's reign. They claim that Cyrus actually was just as bad as other conquerors. Long after he was gone, though, we know from written accounts in several cultures that even his enemies remembered Cyrus as a fair and merciful leader.

RAISED BY WOLVES?

A powerful leader inspires awe. Can this person really be human? Or is he or she superhuman? Part god? In many ancient legends, great leaders have amazing origin stories, just as you'd find in a modern-day comic book or movie. Cyrus has a story like that, too.

The story goes that Cyrus's grandfather, who was a king, had a series of disturbing dreams. When he asked the magi (the wise men at his court) what the dreams could mean, they said that his daughter would have a son who would one day overthrow him.

After Cyrus was born, his grandfather called for a nobleman and ordered him to kill the baby. But, of course, the man couldn't do it. Some stories say that baby Cyrus was raised by someone else. One version says he was raised by a pack of dogs (think Mowgli in *The Jungle Book* or Romulus and Remus, the twins who were cofounders of Rome). There's even a version of the story in which Cyrus is raised by an eagle that found him in the forest.

These stories come from the famed historian Herodotus, who was known to mix mythology into his historical accounts. The idea that a very special person's life must have had an unusual start is popular in cultures around the world.

them captive. Once Cyrus took charge of Babylon, though, he let the Jews go free so they could return to their homeland. This story was so important to the Jewish people that it even appears in the Old Testament of the Bible.

Historians say Cyrus understood that he could never impose one culture, language, or belief system on an empire as large as his. His multicultural empire endured for around two hundred years until Alexander the Great (see page 15) eventually invaded and broke it up.

◄◄ Cyrus's Legacy ►►

Today, Cyrus is admired for showing that a king doesn't have to be brutal and intolerant to be great.

WHEN CYRUS WAS KING...

Buddhism developed in India

the first major river dam was built in China

Chinese philosopher Confucius,
by then an old man, died

the Spartans continued to dominate
the Olympic Games in Greece

ALEXANDER THE GREAT

▲▲▲▲▲▲▲▲▲

GREATEST OF THE GREATS?
(ANCIENT GREECE)

◆

REIGN: 336–323 BCE
FATHER: King Philip II of Macedonia / **MOTHER:** Queen Olympia
SUCCESSOR: The Diadochi (a team of four generals)
OTHER NAMES: Alexander the Accursed, Alexander the Wicked

• • •

WHAT WAS SO GREAT
ABOUT ALEXANDER?

Few leaders are as legendary as Alexander. Within a span of just thirteen years, he built one of the biggest empires ever to exist, stretching two million square miles across three continents. Because his presence was felt in so many cultures, he pops up in legends and stories from around the world going back thousands of years.

GREAT BEGINNINGS

Before he was born, the famous oracle at Delphi, Greece, told Alexander's parents that he would grow up to be an invincible general. Some say a bright star appeared in the sky at his birth, foretelling his successes. These prophecies gave Alexander confidence that he was destined for greatness.

Growing up, Alexander learned from the best: he was tutored by the Greek philosopher Aristotle. He learned to play the lyre and he read a lot of books, committing the contents of works such as *The Iliad* by Homer to memory. People who knew him said Alexander read silently, which was unusual for the time, when almost all reading was done aloud. He was also trained in military arts and horsemanship.

Famously, he trained the untrainable horse Bucephalus when he was just twelve. He later took the horse on his world conquests. During his childhood, he developed friendships with boys who grew up to be his generals and advisors.

Alexander first went into battle with his father when he was eighteen. By the time he was twenty, he was already king.

A GREAT MILITARY STRATEGIST

While his father, King Phillip, had achieved many military victories, Alexander aspired to even more greatness. He put down rebellions in Greek city-states and unified them into one empire. Then he set out to conquer the massive Persian Empire, which he did by the age of twenty-two. After doing that, he declared himself King of Asia. That was a little premature (he still needed to conquer a good number more kingdoms before that would be true). Alexander continued his march east, hoping to reach the Ganges River in India. But after eleven years, his armies refused to go farther. When they reached what's now Pakistan, Alexander returned to Persia, where he died (see page 19).

ECHOES OF ALEXANDER

Even though his conquests took place over the course of just a decade or so, Alexander had a long-term impact on the world. Greek architectural influences can be seen everywhere in the regions he conquered. There are traces of Greek influence in early Buddhism, which was just starting to spread throughout the Indian subcontinent when he got there (some of the edicts of Ashoka [see page 21] were even translated into Greek).

Some say that the green eyes and fair hair seen in Afghan people prove genetic links to Greek soldiers who settled in the area. There's even a group (the Kalash people) in the remote mountains of the region that some call the "lost children of Alexander."

ALEXANDER THE GREAT.
FACT OR FICTION?

•-•-•-•-•-•-•

Because Alexander is such a well-known figure, there are a lot of strange legends about him. But are they true? Read on to find out.

Alexander had two different colored eyes.

True

Alexander had a condition known as heterochromia, which resulted in his having two different eye colors, although accounts vary on which colors.

Alexander named a city after his horse.

True

Alexander and his horse Bucephalus had been together for over a decade when they rode into Alexander's toughest battle ever in what's now Pakistan. While the army was victorious, Bucephalus died. Alexander honored his horse by renaming the city Bucephala.

Macedonia was separate from Greece in Alexander's time.

False

Alexander's kingdom of Macedonia was one of the city-states of Greece. All the city-states had different rulers but a common language and very similar cultures. Alexander brought them all together.

Alexander was compulsively clean.

True

Alexander is said to have taken a bath every day if possible. He shaved before every battle. Those who knew him were surprised at how clean he always smelled considering most people at the time smelled bad.

Alexander was loved by all he conquered.

False

The Persians were not fans of Alexander. He ordered a very important temple destroyed when he took over Persepolis, although he is said to have regretted it later.

Although his army was not the biggest, it was the best for several reasons. Alexander made sure both the men and the animals under his command had enough food and water. The men were well trained. But many attribute his success as a general and ruler to one special tactic: the phalanx. This was a battle formation that his father developed and that Alexander perfected. With this technique, he was able to defeat armies much larger than his while sustaining few casualties.

A GREAT BIG EGO

Anyone who wants to conquer the whole world surely can't be humble, and Alexander was no exception.

He claimed he was the son of Zeus, and his mother backed up his claim. She said that she awoke one night as a bolt of lightning hit her belly, meaning that she had been visited by Zeus. Later, she realized she was expecting Alexander. That heritage also meant he was related to Achilles and Hercules, his battle heroes. He even claimed the shield he carried had belonged to Achilles.

Alexander encouraged artists across the empire to recreate his likeness as a god. People who spoke to him were required to kneel and kiss his hand first.

Alexander the Great

As he moved through the Mediterranean, into Egypt, and then farther east, Alexander founded at least twenty new cities. Because of his big ego (see page 18), he named almost all of them after himself. The best known of these is Alexandria in Egypt, the most important city in the ancient world (it's still the second largest Egyptian city). Because of Alexander's conquests, Greek became the lingua franca, or common language, of the ancient world. Cultures from North Africa to India incorporated parts of Greek culture into their languages, architecture, and more.

ALEXANDER AT THE END

While Alexander was wounded in battle many times, none of those injuries proved fatal. Weeks shy of his thirty-third birthday, he is said to have attended a party at which he drank too much. The next day he was sick. His condition continued to worsen. After ten days suffering with a fever, he died. His cause of death is still a source of speculation. Some say it was alcohol. Others say he was poisoned. Still others say that he may have had malaria or meningitis, which would account for the fever he had during his final days. Perhaps his drinking water had been contaminated.

As Alexander was dying, those around him asked who he would name as his successor. He is said to have replied: "The strongest." No one knew exactly what that meant, so when he did die, his empire was divided among his four top generals (who were also his childhood friends): Cassander, Ptolemy, Antigonus, and Seleucus. They were known as the Diadochi (di-a-DO-key), or "successors."

Even in death, there were prophecies connected to Alexander. It was said that wherever he was buried would become an unconquerable land. That's why his friend Ptolemy is said to have stolen his corpse when it was on the way back to Macedonia and brought it to Egypt, the part of the kingdom that he was given.

Recently, a scholar studying texts from the century after Alexander's death said he thought he had discovered Alexander's will, which indicated he wanted two of his sons to inherit his empire. He also said that the text indicated that Alexander's friends had conspired to poison him. Not everyone agrees with his findings.

Alexander's Legacy

With Alexander's push to rule the world came new connections across continents. More people could understand each other through a shared language (Greek). Some of the cities he founded continue to flourish to this day. Greece influenced culture in the Roman Empire, Asia Minor, and even India. Alexander continues to fascinate us because of his bold vision to rule the world.

WHEN ALEXANDER WAS RULER...

around the Mediterranean Sea, people started using fired bricks instead of mud construction

the Maurya Empire began in India

Romans built the first aqueduct

ASHOKA ·THE· GREAT

A MEMORABLE MONARCH (INDIA)

REIGN: circa 273–232 BCE

FATHER: King Bindusara / **MOTHER:** Queen Devi Dharma

SUCCESSOR: Dasharatha Maurya

OTHER NAMES: Pali Devānaṃpiya (or "The Beloved of the Gods"),
Pali Piyadasī (or "He who regards everyone with affection")

WHAT WAS SO GREAT ABOUT ASHOKA?

Ashoka flipped the script on what was expected of a king. In the past, rulers made laws about what a king's subjects must do for him. Ashoka believed it was the king who had a duty to serve his subjects—and not just the humans in his kingdom, but all living creatures. He made it his life's work to make his kingdom a peaceful, respectful, and compassionate society.

NOT-SO-GREAT BEGINNINGS

Ashoka's grandfather had built the great Maurya dynasty. When Ashoka inherited the throne, there were very few territories left to be conquered in the whole Indian subcontinent. One was Kalinga, a kingdom on the Bay of Bengal. Ashoka sent his armies to invade, resulting in a terrible war that continued for years. Thousands of people died or were taken prisoner. At this time, Ashoka was known as Ashoka the Ferocious. He had no mercy for anyone and had a terrible temper. It's said that he had five hundred of his ministers killed because he thought they were disloyal to him. Ashoka ruled by fear. Even though his empire was the largest in the world at his time, he couldn't be satisfied.

REDISCOVERING ASHOKA

For seven hundred years or so, Ashoka was all but forgotten to people and the history books. Historians in India knew that there were rocks and pillars in different places around the country written in similar scripts. They believed that whoever had written them had wanted to spread a message across the land. But they didn't know how to read the scripts because the languages were no longer understood. In 1836, a Norwegian translator used a coin written in both Greek and Brahmi to finally decode parts of that script. A year later, an Englishman named James Princep (who had been living in India for nearly two decades) used that breakthrough to rediscover the long-vanished language of Kharoshti, which was written in the Brahmi script. (Fun fact: some say Princep was one of history's greatest decoders.) Once he could understand Kharoshti, Princep could read the edicts.

It was almost another hundred years before historians were able to identify Ashoka as the writer of the edicts. Once they knew that Ashoka had written them, they realized that the inscriptions were the oldest understandable writing in India. In this way, Ashoka was rediscovered in 1915 and took his rightful place in India's rich history.

A CHANGE OF HEART

After the Kalinga war, one of Ashoka's advisors introduced him to Buddhism. He became a new person. He is said to have felt great remorse for all his actions of the past and vowed to be different going forward. In Buddhism, nonviolence and compassion are two of the keys to achieving nirvana, or enlightenment (a state of perfect wisdom). Being a Buddhist changed the way Ashoka lived and the way he ruled.

Ashoka's empire was huge. Hundreds of different cultures and faiths coexisted throughout it. There were hunter-gatherers, nomads, farmers, and town dwellers across his lands. His citizens included people who spoke Greek, Aramaic, and dozens of native languages. His people practiced dozens of different religions as well. To keep such a diverse empire together, Ashoka had two choices: he could use armed force to make his people comply with just one unified way of life; or he could come up with social practices that would make all those people feel like they could

ROCK STAR

Ashoka wanted to get the word out about dhamma to all the people in his kingdom. But considering how large his kingdom was, that proved to be a tough job. He needed a way to expose the largest number or people to dhamma, and he hit upon the idea of carving the information into rocks. The rocks would be located in places where large numbers of people could see and read the carvings. Today, the carvings are known as Ashoka's edicts.

The rocks and pillars carved with Ashoka's edicts were positioned throughout what's now India, Nepal, Pakistan, and Afghanistan. While only ten survive today, it's thought that there were more than thirty of them during Ashoka's reign. Some of the pillars were fifty feet high and topped with beautiful carvings of lions or horses; others were simply rocks situated on the ground. They were written in the local languages of their regions, but sometimes more than one language was used on a rock (such as Greek and Aramaic together).

Experts claim that the messages were written by Ashoka himself. They were humble in tone. In many, Ashoka apologized for the Kalinga war and told the people beyond his territory that he was done invading and conquering others. He also wrote that he hoped his children and grandchildren would follow dhamma and not make war. Unfortunately, they didn't follow his wishes. They started wars and their empire fell.

live together in mutual respect, harmony, and trust. Today, we'd call this practice peaceful coexistence. Ashoka called it *dhamma*.

Dhamma can be described as the right way of living. "To do good is difficult," Ashoka said. "One who does good first does something hard to do. Truly, it is easy to do evil." Dhamma was his way of teaching people to do good. Ashoka believed that not just individuals but the government as well should do good. In that way, he could create a peaceful and just society.

So what are the basic concepts of dhamma? They include:

- Don't hurt or kill living beings, including animals.
- Be willing to listen to and learn about the beliefs of others. Let others practice their own religious beliefs.
- Respect your elders and be kind to your friends, teachers, neighbors, servants, and relatives.
- Forgive others, even when harm has been done.
- Be generous to the poor and to your friends and relatives.
- Don't spend too much money; focus on keeping some savings.
- Be compassionate in your treatment of prisoners.
- Don't pursue fame and glory; it's not worth it.
- Don't pursue war.
- Be kind, truthful, loyal, enthusiastic, and pure of heart. Be grateful.
- Reflect on yourself and practice self-control.

Although dhamma was inspired by Ashoka's Buddhist faith, Ashoka didn't favor his religion over others or impose Buddhism on his followers.

Ashoka invited his subjects to contact him at any time, day or night, if they had a problem. He set up tours of his kingdom every five years so he could meet people and understand them better. He formed a team to travel throughout the kingdom to introduce people to dhamma. Under his rule, medical clinics were opened for both people and animals. He and his followers worked for the release and proper treatment of prisoners. They even built roads, dug wells, and planted trees. These infrastructure, human rights, and public health projects made life better for the people of the kingdom.

THE GREAT VEGETARIAN

When Ashoka became a Buddhist, he embraced vegetarianism (not all Buddhists are vegetarian, but many are). He believed that animals' lives were valuable and they should be protected. But he also realized that not all of his subjects would feel the same way. Ashoka outlawed hunting certain animals, killing animals for religious ceremonies, and cruelty to animals. Because of Ashoka, the national symbol of India remains the four lions emblem, which symbolizes power, courage, and confidence. Under the lions there are four other animals: the lion of the north, the elephant of the east, the horse of the south, and the bull of the west.

◀◀ Ashoka's Legacy ▶▶

Unfortunately, Ashoka's heirs didn't follow his way of ruling or the teachings of dhamma. Instead, they started warring with nearby countries and kingdoms. Almost all of the practices of dhamma died out, but some of it carried through to future generations and helped make India the multicultural society it is today. Ashoka also helped Buddhism spread throughout India and into other countries. Today, Ashoka is recognized as a leader who tried to bring people together to live in peace and harmony.

WHEN ASHOKA WAS MONARCH...

Chinese astronomers first observed Halley's comet

Rome was expanding its empire around the Mediterranean

the Maya were just starting to unite into one kingdom in Central America

SUIKO, THE GREAT EMPRESS
JAPAN'S FIRST QUEEN

REIGN: 592–628 CE

FATHER: Emperor Kinmei / **MOTHER:** Kitashi-hime /
HUSBAND: Emperor Bidatsu

SUCCESSOR: Emperor Jomei

• • •

WHAT WAS SO GREAT ABOUT SUIKO?

Empress Suiko opened the door for more women to become rulers of Japan. During her reign, Buddhism expanded, bringing with it much of the culture that the country still embraces today. The idea of Japan as a nation (not just as a collection of separate kingdoms) solidified in her time.

GREAT BEGINNINGS

Suiko was the second daughter of Emperor Kinmei. Her mother was from the prominent Soga clan. Her uncle on the Soga side of the family was especially important in shaping her future. After Suiko's father died, there was a power struggle over who should rule the empire. Suiko's uncle tried to persuade her to take the throne. Suiko said no three times before finally agreeing.

While women had been powerful in Japan before (see page 31), Suiko was the first woman described by historical documents as being emperor, although later she became known as the empress.

NATURE'S PHARMACY

Suiko was concerned with developing medical help for her people. She sent several physicians to China to study their ways of medical treatment. She also brought a Korean doctor to Japan to teach the country's first medical classes.

While the men of her court went hunting, Suiko would lead the women into the forest to search for medicinal plants. She declared that the fifth day of the fifth month would be *kusurigari*, or "medicine hunting" day, when people would collect wild irises and yomogi leaves—used in a tea to promote health and to ward off evil. Today, on May 5 of each year, people in Japan still use yomogi leaves in teas and treats, although the day is now celebrated as Children's Day.

THE LADY EMPEROR

Suiko excelled in both foreign and domestic relations. Early in her reign, she began diplomatic contact with the Chinese empire. This helped the Chinese empire to see Japan as a nation in its own right (rather than just a confederation of separate kingdoms). It also meant that there could be trade between the two kingdoms. Suiko decreed that Japan would use the same lunar calendar that China used and that she would adopt other Chinese systems for use in Japan (see page 30).

Buddhism had been introduced to Japan while her father ruled, but Empress Suiko made it the formal state religion. She invited Buddhist monks and nuns from China and Korea to Japan and commissioned the country's first temples. There were forty-six in all, one of which, Hōryū Temple, still stands today in Nara prefecture. She employed hundreds of monks and nuns to staff the temples and eventually became a Buddhist nun herself. The construction of the temples led to the development of uniquely Japanese forms of Buddhist art, including painting, wood carving, tile making, weaving, and architecture. Buddhist poetry and music developed during her time, too. Even though Buddhism grew in popularity, those who still practiced

Shinto (an ancient Japanese religion) were protected and allowed to continue their beliefs, according to Suiko's royal decrees.

Suiko also made important steps forward in governance (see below). She helped agriculture, too, encouraging the development of irrigation ponds for rice farming. Empress Suiko died after she had been empress for thirty-five years. She may have been the first woman to rule Japan, but thanks to her success, she certainly wasn't the last (see page 32).

A FEATHER IN HER CAP

During Suiko's reign, the Twelve-Level Cap and Rank system was introduced in Japan. Before this system was developed, a person's job was based on the family they had been born into. If you were the son of a farmer, you'd be a farmer. If you were a noble, you could expect the best jobs to be available to you. But this new system meant people could be promoted due to job performance, and not just because of family connections or history.

The cap system was modeled after a system from China and the kingdom that would later be known as Korea. The system was based on six qualities, with two levels (lesser and greater) in each: knowledge, justice, sincerity, propriety, benevolence, and virtue. A person would start at the bottom (lesser knowledge) and work his way up through the system, getting promoted to the next level and working toward greater virtue, which was at the top.

For each level, the official was given a cap in a color that would indicate the level:

Knowledge, black   Propriety, red

Justice, white   Benevolence, blue

Sincerity, yellow   Virtue, purple

The caps were made of silk, with silver and gold embroidery, and embellished with a feather.

Empress Suiko's ambassador to China started out with a deep red cap and then made it all the way up to deep purple. The cap system helped to show that Japanese society at the time placed high value on these virtues, and anyone—not just nobles—could achieve them.

LIVING IN HARMONY

Suiko might be best known for the Seventeen-Article Constitution, which was introduced during her reign. This was Japan's first constitution. Unlike modern constitutions, though, it was more about ideals than laws. In Suiko's time, the government was largely focused on trying to avoid conflicts before they happened rather than resolving them after they occurred.

Suiko's constitution was based on principles developed by the Chinese philosopher Confucius. Translated, it goes something like this:

> *Value harmony and avoid disputes. No one can avoid being influenced by their class and upbringing. Not many people are truly wise. Therefore, there is a lot of conflict—in families, within communities, and between neighboring villages. But when those in the upper classes value harmony and those in the lower classes are friendly, they can get along and make progress together.*

The constitution goes on to state that officials must put aside their personal feelings when making decisions that affect the public and that an important decision can't be made by only one person. It was the beginning of a fairer and more honest way of governing.

THE WOMEN OF THE CHRYSANTHEMUM THRONE

I n Japan, the reigning monarch is said to hold the Chrysanthemum Throne. There *is* an actual throne in the Imperial Palace in Kyoto (used only for ceremonies), but "to hold the Chrysanthemum Throne" is more of an expression that means to be the head of state. In 2019, Emperor Naruhito became the 126th emperor to hold the throne.

Empress Suiko was the 33rd. While she is recognized as the first true empress, there are women of legend who may or may not have held the throne before her. Empress Himiko, for example, was said to have reigned from 189 to 248 CE. She was thought to have been a sorceress who lived in a palace guarded by a thousand female guards. It was said that she was descended from the sun goddess Amaterasu. However, because what's known about her comes from China, and not Japan, she's thought to be legendary rather than real.

Empress Jingu is also considered to be semi-legendary. She was a warrior queen who is said to have led an army on a three-year campaign in what's now Korea around the year 200 CE.

There have been seven empresses in Japan since Empress Suiko. Empress Kogyoku was said to have magical powers. She performed a ritual that was reported to have brought rain when there was a drought. Empress Jitō was known to be a poet. Empress Genmei commissioned the first written history about Japan. Empress Genshō was the first woman to inherit the throne from her mother, while Empress Meishō was the first ruler of the Edo period, the time in Japanese history when the imperial family became very strong. Go-Sakuramachi was the last Japanese woman to serve as empress. She abdicated the throne in favor of her nephew in 1813. Sadly, in 1889, women in Japan lost the right to hold the throne, and they still haven't gotten it back.

◀◀ Suiko's Legacy ▶▶

Suiko established Buddhism as an official religion of Japan, which influenced every aspect of society, from the arts to food. Her reign also made it possible for other women to take the role of female emperor well into the nineteenth century.

WHEN SUIKO WAS EMPRESS...

the plague was raging all over the Roman Empire

construction began on The Temple of Inscriptions in the Mayan city of Palenque (see page 35)

the expression "God bless you" was decreed by Pope Gregory to be the official response to someone sneezing; this was believed to help prevent the spread of bubonic plague that was raging across Europe

PACAL the GREAT

A MAJOR MAYA
(CENTRAL AMERICA)

REIGN: 615–683

FATHER: K'an Mo' Hix / **MOTHER:** Lady Sak K'uk'

SUCCESSOR: K'inich Kan Bahlam II (Radiant Snake Jaguar)

OTHER NAMES: K'Inich Janab Pakal, King of Kings,
Lord Pacal, 8 Ahau, Sun Shield

• • •

WHAT WAS SO GREAT ABOUT PACAL?

Pacal was responsible for some of the greatest art, architecture, and engineering in

his time—and in all of Mayan civilization. These achievements were possible thanks

THE LOST CITY

Palenque was abandoned and lost in the jungle for almost a thousand years. When Spanish explorer Ramon de Ordonez y Aguilar rediscovered it in 1773, there was a lot of speculation about the city's origin. Because they didn't believe that the indigenous people of Central America could have been advanced enough to create the city, the Spanish came up with outlandish theories. Perhaps the amazing temples and pyramids had been built by the ancient Egyptians who had crossed the ocean in "big canoes," or by survivors from the lost city of Atlantis. We now know what the early Spanish colonizers didn't: that the Maya were one of the most sophisticated ancient cultures in the world.

to the peace and stability he brought to his kingdom. The stories recorded in stone carvings in Pacal's city of Palenque helped preserve Mayan culture long after this civilization had vanished.

MAYA FEVER!

In 1839, the adventurers John Stephens (an American) and Frederick Catherwood (from Britain) slogged and hacked their way through the Mexican and Guatemalan jungles on an expedition. They were looking at forty-four different Mayan sites, including Palenque. They even bought the entire ancient city of Copan for $50 with the hopes of taking it apart and sending it to the United States on a boat so they could put it in museums (until they realized how heavy it was).

When Stephens and Catherwood returned to the United States, they wrote a nine-hundred-page book about their adventure. It became one of the world's first international bestsellers. That's when Mayan fever took hold in Europe and America. People wanted to read, see, and hear everything they could about the mysterious Mayan civilization. After a few years the fervor for all-things Mayan died down. Amazon-mania became the next craze. But Stephens and Catherwood's adventure drew attention to the Mayan culture so that future archeologists could study and learn from it. The increased attention to Mayan civilization eventually led to the rediscovery of Pacal's tomb.

A MIGHTY MAYA

Imagine a great city of limestone pyramids, temples, and palaces surrounded by dense, lush jungle. You see aqueducts that bring water from an underground stream and tall towers for astronomers to watch the skies. The sounds of macaws and howler monkeys can be heard echoing through the canopy of the nearby forest. This was Palenque at its height, the city ruled by the mighty Pacal.

THE HIDDEN STAIRCASE

Archeologist Alberto Ruz Lhuillier was working on the Temple of Inscriptions in 1948 when he noticed something unusual. Part of the floor wasn't like the rest—there were two rows of holes with plugs in them in one section. The walls didn't end at the floor as in the rest of the room. Lhuillier worked to remove the plugs and discovered the start of a secret underground staircase. The staircase was blocked with huge stones and dirt. It took four years to clear all of it away and, finally, in 1952, his team was able to access the seventy-two steps leading down to another blocked door, then another and another. At each blocked door, there were curious items that led the archeological team to believe it was on the trail of an important discovery: a box of jade beads, six human skulls, and red painted shells. Finally, beyond the third door, they discovered Pacal's tomb. It hadn't been opened in more than a thousand years!

Inside, they found Pacal's coffin, with his remains still inside. For the archeologists, it was like discovering King Tut's tomb: a once-in-a-century find.

PACAL'S HEAVENLY HOTLINE

Pacal was buried under the Temple of the Inscriptions. He was laid to rest wearing a mosaic mask made from hundreds of pieces of jade, plus lots of other jewelry. But he was too important to just bury and forget. His tomb was designed with a speaking tube that led from an upper platform of the temple down to his sarcophagus. When there was a problem, the priests of the court would speak into the tube to ask him for advice from beyond the grave.

PACAL, THE ANCIENT ASTRONAUT?

fter Pacal's tomb was uncovered in 1952, the world experienced Mayan fever all over again. No one had deciphered the Mayan writing system yet, so people were taking wild guesses about what all those symbols in the Temple of the Inscriptions meant.

In 1968, Erich von Däniken wrote a book called *Chariots of the Gods: Unsolved Mysteries of the Past*. In the book, he proposed that many ancient civilizations, including the Maya, had been visited by ancient extraterrestrial astronauts and that they were welcomed as gods. He thought the pictorial scene on Pacal's sarcophagus lid showed the king taking off in a space ship or possibly on an early form of motorcycle. As crazy as his premise was, the book became a bestseller.

In the 1980s, a team finally cracked the code of the Mayan glyphs and started to translate them. It turned out that the picture was really a representation of Pacal falling backward into the underworld, where he would be reborn as a god.

Even if it's a bit wacky, the spaceship theory caught people's attention and increased interest in Mayan culture once again. The interest generated helped make preserving Palenque a priority so that it will be visited and appreciated by future generations.

THE END OF THE WORLD AS WE KNOW IT?

The Mayans followed a calendar system that had been used by cultures before them in Central America. This system had different ways of counting time. The *Tzolkin* was a 260-day calendar with 20 periods of 13 days each. This calendar was used to determine the time of religious ceremonies.

They also had a 365-day solar calendar, but instead of 12 months like we currently use, their calendar had 18 months of 20 days each and one month that is only five days long. The third calendar was the Long Count calendar for the universal cycle—about 5,125 years long. The Maya believed that the universe was destroyed and then recreated at the start of each universal cycle. The last date on the most recent Long Count calendar was December 21, 2012. Some people believed that this meant the world was going to end that day.

A poll showed that one in ten people had anxiety about the fate of the world that year. Some even prepared for the end of the world. Of course, in reality, life went on. (According to ancient Mayan time, we're now living in the early years of a new world.)

When Pacal came to power at the age of twelve, Mayan civilization had already been in existence for more than a thousand years. The Maya had a written language (called glyphs), art, and mathematics. They were skilled in astronomy, too. In the early days of his reign, Pacal helped rebuild Palenque (which was then known by its Mayan name of Lakhma, or "Big Water") after it had been devastated by multiple wars. He raised an army to defend his city and sent his enemies a message by taking prisoners from invading armies and sacrificing them to the gods. His plan to project an image of strength worked, and rival cities decreased their attacks on Palenque. The relative peace allowed Pacal to begin working on what he is best known for today: Palenque's incredible buildings.

Although there was already a palace in the city when Pacal came into power, he expanded it to include inner courtyards and corridors, creating a breathtaking complex. He commissioned carvings that celebrated the city's military victories. Pacal oversaw the creation of an underground channel to bring water to the city—a remarkable feat of engineering for the time. He had the Temple of the Inscriptions built as high as a modern ten-story building. Although it wasn't finished until after he died, he even had his own tomb built inside the massive temple.

 Pacal's Legacy

Pacal had the longest reign of any king in the Americas and the fourth longest of any monarch in history! He is the best known of all Mayan kings, and the city of Palenque is now one of the most popular tourist destinations in Mexico.

WHEN PACAL WAS KING...

Mohammad began preaching Islam, and the religion spread rapidly throughout what's now called the Middle East, Central Asia, Southeast Asia, and present-day India

paper money was developed in China

the game *chatrang* (which later developed into chess) was invented in Persia

the world population reached about 50 million

GOOD KING WENCESLAS

REIGN: circa 921–935

FATHER: Vratislav I, Duke of Bohemia / **MOTHER:** Drahomira

SUCCESSOR: Boleslav the Cruel, Duke of Bohemia

OTHER NAMES: Václav the Good

• • •

WHAT WAS SO GREAT ABOUT KING WENCESLAS?

How did a Czech duke with a very hard-to-pronounce name (it's WHEN-ces-loss) end up being remembered as a king in a popular English Christmas song? Much of what we know about Wenceslas comes from legend, but it's clear that he's become a symbol for helping the poor and those in need. His examples of generosity and peacekeeping have made him memorable through the ages.

BEING GOOD IN BAD TIMES

To set the record straight, Wenceslas was never a king. He was a duke. His Czech name wasn't even Wenceslas—it was Václav. In Czech, he's called Václav I or Václav the Good.

Wenceslas was born in a difficult time. There was conflict in his kingdom of Bohemia (part of the Holy Roman Empire, which developed after the fall of Rome). Some nobles wanted an alliance with what's now Germany. Wenceslas's family was in conflict, too. His father died when he was only thirteen years old. Wenceslas became

ruler after his father's death, but his mother was appointed his regent. While she was regent, she had his grandmother killed because of their religious differences. Finally, upon his eighteenth birthday, Wenceslas took over the throne.

EXTREME SIBLING RIVALRY!

Fights between siblings can sometimes get out of hand. Insults fly, threats are made, and sometimes even worse happens. But in the past, if you were royalty and an empire was at stake, sibling rivalry could get *much* worse. Wenceslas and his brother Boleslav weren't the only siblings in a deadly royal rivalry.

Tales of brothers killing brothers are as old as time. According to the Bible, the very first brothers in existence were at each other's throats—and it was Cain who killed his younger brother, Abel, in a jealous fit. You may also have heard of Romulus and Remus, twin brothers of famous Roman myth. One version of their story says Romulus killed Remus by hitting him on the head with a rock during an argument about building the city of Rome.

Things were especially bad if you happened to be a boy in the Ottoman royal family. Whoever was first in line for the throne would have his rival relatives (which could include brothers, cousins, or nephews) imprisoned in a lovely but inescapable cage to decrease the chance of an assassination plot (see page 137). Whenever the ruler had an heir of his own lined up, he would make sure the other males in the family were strangled with a silk cord to eliminate any competition.

And what about royal sisters? Since girls weren't usually allowed to inherit the throne, they would rarely resort to such drastic measures; at worst, a sister might be banished or sent into exile (but you can read about the rivalry between England's Mary Tudor and Elizabeth I on page 77).

BEHIND THE MUSIC:
THE STORY OF "GOOD KING WENCESLAS"

M ost people outside the Czech Republic only know of Wenceslas because of the song "Good King Wenceslas," written in 1853 by the English hymn writer and reverend John Mason Neal.

Neal worked with the poor, managing an almshouse (a kind of charity center). In his spare time, he wrote music. Although there were many Christmas carols in the nineteenth century, he wanted to write a song for Boxing Day, celebrated on December 26 in England and other countries. (Boxing Day is the feast day of St. Stephen, a day when—in English tradition—money is collected for the poor.)

Years before, Neal had read an English translation of a Czech poem about Wenceslas. He thought Wenceslas's reputation for giving to the poor made him a perfect subject for a Boxing Day song.

Neal used the melody from a song called "Tempus adest floridum" ("It is the time of flowering") to create his Boxing Day carol. When "Good King Wenceslas" was first published, not everyone loved it, but somehow it has stood the test of time. It has been recorded by musicians from the Beatles to REM.

During Wenceslas's reign, there were still slaves in his kingdom, a holdover practice from the Roman Empire. It is said that, as duke Wenceslas bought all the slaves their freedom and gave food, clothing, and firewood to the poor. He did his good works in the middle of the night—in bare feet, even if it was snowing—so that no one would be ashamed to be seen accepting help. He also visited prisoners to make sure they were not badly treated.

But not everyone was happy with Wenceslas's actions. His brother Boleslav wasn't a fan. After Wenceslas had been duke for only ten years, he was stabbed just

Neal's song goes like this:

Good King Wenceslas looked out on the feast of Stephen,
When the snow lay round about, deep and crisp and even;
Brightly shone the moon that night, though the frost was cruel,
When a poor man came in sight, gath'ring winter fuel.
"Hither, page, and stand by me, if thou know'st it, telling
Yonder peasant, who is he? Where and what his dwelling?"
"Sire, he lives a good league hence, underneath the mountain,
Right against the forest fence, by Saint Agnes' fountain."
"Bring me flesh and bring me wine, bring me pine logs hither,
Thou and I will see him dine, when we bear them thither."
Page and monarch forth they went, forth they went together,
Through the rude wind's wild lament and the bitter weather.
"Sire, the night is darker no, and the wind blows stronger;
Fails my heart, I know not how, I can go no longer."
"Mark my footsteps, good my page, tread thou in them boldly:
Thou shalt find the winter's rage freeze thy blood less coldly."
In his master's steps he trod, where the snow lay dinted;
Heat was in the very sod which the Saint had printed.
Therefore, Christian men, be sure, wealth or rank possessing,
Ye who now will bless the poor shall yourselves find blessing.

as he was going into church one night. Stories differ on who held the knife (was it his brother or someone hired to do the dirty deed?). Either way, it's certain that Boleslav was responsible.

WAITING FOR WENCESLAS

Wenceslas was ruler for only a decade, but he has become one of the most important figures in Czech history. He showed the Czech people what a good king does and acts like.

Not long after his death, word of Wenceslas's goodness started to spread around Europe, and it was the Holy Roman Emperor (the title for leaders in Rome after the empire broke up) who gave Wenceslas the title of king after his death.

Wenceslas was also made a saint—the patron saint of his country. His feast day—a national holiday—is celebrated on September 28 each year. One of the main squares in the city of Prague is named Wenceslas Square. In the square there's a statue of Duke Wenceslas on a horse. His tomb in St. Vitus Cathedral is a popular tourist destination.

There is a legend that, even today, Wenceslas is sleeping with an army of knights under Mount Blanik, about thirty-five miles from Prague. When the country needs him most (the legend says), he will awaken and he and his army will ride out to save the country and bring eternal peace.

Another legend claims that in the moment of greatest danger, his statue in Wenceslas Square will come to life and the good ruler will raise the army sleeping under the mountain.

◄◄ Wenceslas's Legacy ►►

Although he had a short reign, Wenceslas's goodness is a matter of national pride for the Czech people.

WHEN WENCESLAS WAS KING...

the first use of gunpowder for military purposes
was recorded in China

the Kingdom of England was united

the Ghana Empire in West Africa was at its peak

SEJONG •THE• GREAT

A SERIOUS SCHOLAR (KOREA)

REIGN: 1418–1450

FATHER: King Taejong / **MOTHER:** Consort Min /
SIBLINGS: Prince Yangnyeong and Prince Hyoryeong
OTHER NAMES: Chungnyeong, the Great Scholar

• • •

WHAT WAS SO GREAT ABOUT SEJONG?

Sejong did something no one had done before: invented an alphabet from scratch. Hangul, the Korean alphabet, has been called one of the greatest inventions in all of history. His support for science led to world-changing advancements in agriculture and astronomy. His social policies, such as an early form of family leave, acknowledged the important role government can play in social issues.

GREAT BEGINNINGS

As a child, Sejong was the ultimate bookworm. He read everything he could get his hands on. In the same way modern parents take a kid's phone or video games away because he or she is spending too much time on them, Sejong's father, King Taejong, is said to have hidden his son's books so that he would do something—*anything*—other than read. But King Taejong admired how hard Sejong studied, especially compared with his oldest brother, Yangnyeong, who spent all his time drinking, flirting with women, and hunting. It's said Yangnyeong didn't really want to be king, so he played up his bad behavior. He even skipped his required "prince lessons." Sejong's middle brother, Prince Hyoryeong, didn't want to be king, either, so he left home to become a Buddhist monk. That put Sejong in the position to inherit

the throne, and King Taejong had confidence that he could do it. When his father died, Sejong became king.

GOLDEN YEARS

Sejong was a big-picture thinker who believed that society would be better if everyone could read and gain more knowledge.

He also believed that everyone, no matter their class, should have a chance to succeed. "How can a king—who should rule over all people and all things in the country with impartiality—treat those of low birth any differently from the way he treats others?" he asked. He allowed people from all social classes the opportunity to work in government, even though those jobs only went to the upper classes in the past.

Sejong also established the Hall of Worthies (also known as the Jade Hall), a royal research institute. Here, his top scholars worked on history, geography, astronomy, math, agriculture, and more. At that time, Korea used the Chinese calendar. It was geared toward the longitude of the Chinese capital, so everything was a little off in terms of timing. Sejong directed his astronomers to create new and improved sundials and to develop a new calendar so that the time keeping would be accurate in Korea. They also created new astronomical maps and celestial globes, and invented the orrery, a mechanical model of the solar system that demonstrates how the planets move.

Although he wasn't really a war-loving king, Sejong's interest in science led to the invention of new types of cannons and fire-arrows. By far, though, the most important scientific invention by his "worthies" was the rain gauge. Before its invention, no one had thought of measuring rainfall. It was a breakthrough invention for improving agriculture across the country (and eventually the world).

You could say Sejong was the inventor of family leave policies. He insisted that both parents have time off of work after a baby was born. Mothers got a hundred days paid leave! Sejong worked to improve the justice system, too. People accused of major crimes were allowed three appeals. Those who wanted to appeal could beat a drum outside the palace to ask for a hearing. Sejong insisted that prisons be kept clean and warm so disease wouldn't spread and he insisted that prisoners had to be fed three meals a day.

Sejong's reign was called a Golden Age in Korean history and helped make Korea the leading nation it is today.

A GREAT LISTENER

One of Sejong's great strengths was his ability to listen. "Leading a sheltered existence inside a palace," he said, "I am not aware of all the goings-on among the people. If there are any matters that cause anguish to the people, you should report them to me without failing." He also said that "a wise ruler should not neglect minority opinions and give a careful hearing. It would be foolish for a monarch to

IT'S NOT ME; IT'S YOU

One of the great things about Sejong is that he knew his success wasn't because of his own personal genius. He was open to learning and grateful for help. "All that I am, or will be, I have learned from my family, my friends, my teachers," he is quoted as saying. He also knew that his own success depended on the people of his kingdom: "If the people prosper, how can the king not prosper with them? And if the people do not prosper, how may the king prosper without them?" This belief is something that many great leaders have in common: success in ruling a country is not just because of them; it's due to everyone.

INVENTING THE ALPHABET

— — — — — — —

The Korean people had their own language for more than a thousand years, but they used the Chinese alphabet to write it. There were tens of thousands of Chinese characters to learn, and these characters didn't match the sounds in Korean words. This made communication complicated. Sejong commented, in 1443, that using Chinese characters for Korean was "like trying to fit a square handle into a round hole."

Sejong believed strongly that the Korean language needed its own alphabet. "The sounds of our nation's language are so different from those of China that they cannot be represented adequately with Chinese characters," he said. "Many people cannot express themselves when they want to put their feelings into writing. I have been very distressed by this."

So Sejong got his best scholars working on a solution to this problem. He was constantly scribbling notes about it. People said he was a little obsessed.

Not everyone loved the idea of creating an alphabet specifically for the Korean language. The upper classes liked being the only ones who had unlimited access to knowledge through their ability to read. They thought the Chinese alphabet was more refined and considered the new alphabet vulgar. Plus, they didn't want to have to change all their documents to a new writing system. But Sejong ignored all these complaints and eventually finished the new alphabet.

The Korean alphabet is called Hangul. In Hangul, the characters represent sound syllables grouped together.

In 1443, the new alphabet was ready: it consisted of twenty-eight letters with seventeen consonants and eleven vowels. It was said that the smartest people could learn it in a few hours and even the foolish would understand in only ten days. Sejong's team claimed that even the sound of the wind, the call of a crane, or the barking of a dog could all be written in Hangul. "I have newly devised twenty-eight letters, which I hope everyone will learn easily and use daily," Sejong announced. Sejong had poems, religious texts, farming books, and well-known proverbs translated into Hangul so his entire country could have access to them. (Fun fact: language experts today state that Hangul is the most perfect alphabet ever invented.)

make decisions based on a single person's opinion." Sejong knew that being a good listener is one of the top qualities for being a good leader, and he excelled at this throughout his reign.

Understanding injustice in his kingdom was an essential part of doing a good job, Sejong believed. "How can a king hope to live up to the dignity expected of him as a ruler when he refuses to hear out his people when they bring to his attention injustices done to him?" he wrote. His attention to their concerns made Sejong a beloved leader among his subjects.

◄◄ Sejong's Legacy ►►

The Korean alphabet lives on. Today you can see King Sejong on Korea's 10,000-won currency note and there are statues of him all over Korea. There's even a King Sejong video game!

WHEN SEJONG WAS KING...

Joan of Arc began to lead an army in France

the building of the Forbidden City in Beijing was completed

the Aztec and Incan empires were at their peak in Central and South America

ships from Europe began to sail around the world,
sparking the Age of Discovery

ASKIA THE GREAT

THE SONGHAI SUPERPOWER
(TIMBUKTU, SONGHAI EMPIRE)

REIGN: 1493–1529

FATHER: Arlum Silla / **MOTHER:** Kassai

SUCCESSOR: Askia Monzo Musa

REAL NAME: Mohamed Touré

WHAT WAS SO GREAT ABOUT ASKIA?

Askia helped to unify many diverse cultures in West Africa at a time when they had long been fighting. The peace and stability that developed during his reign led to a Golden Age in his kingdom. Commerce across the vast region of West Africa thrived during his reign, and he was instrumental in the spread of Islam.

GREAT BY CHOICE

Askia wasn't supposed to be king. He started as a general in the army of Soni Ali—the leader who had built the Songhai Empire. Ali had a reputation as a cruel king. When Ali died, his unpopular son took over and the country was thrown into turmoil. Askia knew he could rule better, so with the support of the people, he defeated Ali's son and became king.

As king, Askia expanded the empire all the way to the Atlantic Ocean. It became the largest empire in the history of the African continent, as big as modern-day Europe.

People from many different cultures lived in Songhai. Keeping such a vast empire together was no easy task. Askia created a central government with ministries overseeing areas such as commerce, army, navy, taxes, and the treasury.

He also appointed mayors and governors across the kingdom. His diplomatic corps invited ambassadors from other kingdoms to come to Songhai and encouraged scholars from around the world to move to his capital city, Timbuktu. It became an international center of learning and trade (see below).

Askia helped develop Sankore University in Timbuktu. At its height, there were around 25,000 students at the university studying in one of four different colleges.

SEE YOU IN TIMBUKTU

Nowadays, if someone wants to indicate that something is very far away and hard to get to, they might say, "From here to Timbuktu." But do you know anything about the real Timbuktu? It's a city located in present-day Mali. But in Askia's time it was one of the most exciting cities in the world. It was called the Athens of Africa because it was a major center of knowledge. It was also called the Mecca of the Sahara because it was an Islamic spiritual center. A French explorer who visited during Askia's time said it was one of the most amazing places he'd ever seen. There were hotels and restaurants for travelers and at night, there were people playing music and dancing in the streets until after midnight, according to one visitor's record.

Located at a major crossroads for the desert caravans (see below) and on the banks of the Niger River, Timbuktu was called the place where the canoe and the camel met. Timbuktu was truly a melting pot of cultures. Trade brought people from all over North Africa to the city. Because so many people met and exchanged ideas there, Timbuktu also became a very important place to the spread of Islam. There was an important mosque in the city.

As sea travel began to become more popular, trade shifted to coastal towns, and Timbuktu began to be forgotten. But today, Timbuktu is a UNESCO World Heritage site, recognized as a place incredibly important to world history.

THE TRANS—SAHARAN SUPERHIGHWAY

Imagine caravans stretching miles long, traveling through the Sahara for months at a time, bringing precious goods and practical items to new markets across the desert.

Salt, gold, ivory, kola nuts, cloth, beads, glass, ceramics, and gemstones: these are just a few of the items that were traded in Timbuktu during Askia's time. There was no currency back then, so traders bartered or used pieces of gold.

Caravan journeys could cover 1,000 miles or more and take several months to complete. There were routes that started as far north and east as Tunis on the Mediterranean Sea, linking to other routes coming toward Timbuktu. While the average caravan would have included around 1,000 camels, there are reports of caravans with as many as 12,000 camels! Askia himself led a caravan this large to Mecca.

Caravan travel wasn't easy, however. The temperatures in the desert were extreme—blistering heat during the day, freezing at night. The organizers of the caravan would have to identify oases along the way and try to keep good time to make sure they were able to reach the next stop before running out of water. Trade would take place not just in the cities, but in the oases, too. That's why Askia took control of the major oases.

Caravan travel could be very dangerous. Raiders would hide and ambush travelers, stealing their goods. Because of the remoteness of the desert, there would be no way for those who had been robbed to reclaim their goods.

Although there are good roads in the Sahara today, some travelers still take camels to cut distances or go to hard-to-reach places. They carry solar-powered electronics and can use satellite mapping, though, so they don't need scouts to find their next oasis!

DESERT LIBRARIES

In Askia's time, books were luxury items. Books from all over were brought to Timbuktu to be traded. Everyone wanted them, so they were expensive. There were books on topics ranging from science to poetry.

Some books were written in Arabic and some were written in African languages using the Arabic script. Even though many of the books were written elsewhere, there was also a major book copying industry in Timbuktu.

With so many books, there were a lot of libraries—maybe as many as one hundred in Timbuktu. Some of the smaller libraries in the city had more than a thousand books in their buildings. There were more books in Timbuktu than any place in the world during Askia's reign.

When the Moroccan army invaded Timbuktu in 1591, they burned many of the libraries, destroying the books. They brought some books back to Morocco, where they stayed until it was colonized by France. Then some of the books were taken to France and put into museums. For centuries in Timbuktu, local people kept books in private homes or hidden in caves to protect them. Some of them were rare illuminated manuscripts, dating back as far as the thirteenth century.

In 2012, the books were once again threatened by war. A group of soldiers seized books at one of Timbuktu's historic libraries because they didn't like what the books said. They threw them in a bonfire. But a librarian in Timbuktu was able smuggle thousands of books out of the country to save them. Once the fighting in the area was over, the books were moved back. It's estimated that there are between 200,000 and 300,000 books in the library today!

Courses offered included philosophy, religion, science, navigation, astronomy, medicine, architecture, engineering, and more. Scholars came from all over the Islamic world to teach there.

Askia is said to have gone on a pilgrimage to Mecca, bringing with him a caravan of 1,500 soldiers and carrying 300,000 pieces of gold. This display of power and wealth impressed people and leaders along the way and cemented his reputation as a man of great stature.

◄◄ **Askia's Legacy** ►►

Askia is remembered for spreading Islam and increasing trade with Europe and Asia. His support for scribes and scholars and the books they wrote made it possible for us to understand more about African history today.

WHEN ASKIA WAS KING...

the Spanish began exploring the Americas

trade on a global scale began to take off

the Ottoman Empire conquered Egypt

LORENZO *the* MAGNIFICENT

THE MARVELOUS MEDICI
(RENAISSANCE FLORENCE)

REIGN: 1449–1492

FATHER: Piero the Gouty / **MOTHER:** Lucrezia Tornabuoni

SUCCESSOR: Piero the Unfortunate

WHAT WAS SO GREAT ABOUT LORENZO?

Lorenzo believed that it was important to ask big questions and to try to learn as much as possible about the world. He believed art was important, not just to individuals, but also to society. By placing importance on the arts, Lorenzo enriched not only the lives of people in his own country during his time but also the lives of those throughout history who still appreciate the art created through his sponsorship.

MAGNIFICENT BEGINNINGS

Lorenzo was born into one of the most powerful families—the Medicis—in Florence, which was one of the richest cities in the world at that time. For more than a hundred years, the Medici family had gained wealth and influence. They had many palaces all over Tuscany—the area of Italy where they ruled (this was before the different parts of Italy were unified into one country).

When Lorenzo was born, the world was changing. The Dark Ages (the period after the Roman Empire fell, when few people were educated) were over. The Renaissance (a time when science, education, and the arts began to thrive again) was starting. As he was growing up, Lorenzo was educated by the brightest minds of his generation. He studied philosophy. He learned to speak Greek and Latin and to

play the lute. He was also an excellent jouster. Is it any wonder that he was destined to become magnificent?

MAGNIFICENT POWER

Imagine a high-ceilinged room in a palace, decorated with elaborate frescos and bronze and marble sculptures. Here, a group of well-dressed courtiers are discussing big ideas, such as "What is the nature of life?" and "What is love?" Some of the most legendary artists in the world come in and out—Leonardo da Vinci, Sandro Botticelli, and Michelangelo Buonarroti. This was Lorenzo's court at its peak.

Lorenzo was one of the greatest supporters of the arts in his time. The famous painter and sculptor Michelangelo even lived with him for a while! He was also known as a great entertainer. He held masked balls at his palace. He was known to keep many exotic pets at his country home, including a giraffe that was given to him as a gift from a ruler in North Africa.

BLOODY SUNDAY

Lorenzo brought a lot of great things to Florence, but he didn't always do it in the nicest way. He earned many enemies, including members of the Pazzi family, who wanted to take the Medici's power. On Easter Sunday in 1478, members of the Pazzi family ambushed Lorenzo and his brother Giuliano as they went to mass at Florence's main cathedral. During the most holy part of the service, the Pazzis attacked. Lorenzo was only slightly wounded, but Giuliano died. Legend has it you can still see his blood stains on the cathedral's floor.

The pope was on the Pazzis' side, and shortly after the attack he banished Lorenzo from the Catholic Church. The King of Naples sided with the pope and soon invaded Florence. In order to protect his people, Lorenzo sailed to Naples and offered himself as prisoner to stop the invasion. Because of his political skill, he was able to negotiate his way out and preserve the independence of his realm.

MORE MEDICI MURDERS

W hat happened to Giuliano at the Duomo was probably the most famous murder story of the Medici family. But it wasn't the only one.

Isabella, daughter of Cosimo de' Medici I, married Paolo Orsini when she was just sixteen years old. When she died at age thirty-four, her husband said she had fallen while washing her hair, but others said that he strangled her in front of witnesses. Strangely, her cousin Leonora had died of the same kind of accident at the same house a few days earlier. She is also thought to have been strangled by her husband.

Francesco de' Medici chose for his second wife a woman named Bianca Capello, who came from Venice. People in Florence accused her of being a spy or a witch. Francesco's brother Ferdinando is thought to have had both of them poisoned at their country house: they died within days of each other in 1587. Perhaps it was karma; Francesco is said to have known about and approved of Isabella's and Leonora's murders.

Lorenzo was an enthusiastic reader. His family had many books, but he collected even more by sending out agents to find and purchase the most important books on the continent. He started a library that still exists in Florence today, the Biblioteca Laurenziana (roughly translated, it means "Lorenzo's Library"). He improved relations with other kingdoms in Italy and even used art as a tool for diplomacy. He sent his favored architects and artists to other courts to offer their services. This promoted Florence's reputation as a cultural center and built goodwill. Florence's well-known artists and skilled craftspeople gained were offered greater opportunities.

Lorenzo was very well respected by his citizens. When he died, it was said that lightning struck the top of the Duomo (the cathedral of Florence) and that the lion statues in the city came to life and began to fight each other. He was so memorable that even today there are stories of his ghost haunting the city.

RENAISSANCE MEN (AND WOMEN)

You may have heard someone being called a "Renaissance Man." That expression is often used to describe a person who can do just about everything—and do it well. The term was coined to describe people like Leonardo da Vinci, who did everything from painting the *Mona Lisa* to inventing a flying machine.

Leonardo was remarkable, but his range of knowledge wasn't completely out of the ordinary for his time. Educated noblemen in Renaissance Italy were expected to study Latin and Greek, philosophy, natural science, astronomy, music, history, drama, and poetry. They needed to understand art and architecture. But they also had to be strong. They studied archery, swordplay, jousting, and hunting. In addition to all of this, they were expected to have good manners, to be able to carry on a decent conversation, and to dance well. There was no such thing as specializing in Lorenzo's day: you had to be good at *everything*.

Life was different for girls, though. They weren't allowed to leave the house without their father, brother, or another older male to look out for them. They were often taught poetry, music, and dancing at home. They were expected to be good conversation partners. But science and fine arts were off limits to them. Despite this, some women became very powerful. Isabella d'Este, for example, became known as "the first lady of the world." She ruled her town of Mantua, first when her husband was imprisoned, and again before her son was old enough to take over for his father. She used her family's money to support artists, including Michelangelo and Leonardo da Vinci. Some think she may have even been the model for the *Mona Lisa*!

Even though they couldn't take apprenticeships required of artists, some girls in Renaissance Italy studied with private tutors to become artists. Sofonisba Anguissola, for example, became well known and was invited to be a court painter in Spain. Lavinia Fontana was trained by her father, who was also a painter. Renaissance girls had the talent, but they had to work harder to get the respect that men got.

AN AMAZING ART COLLECTION

Leonardo. Michelangelo. Botticelli. These are some of the best-known names in art. And much of their work started out in the Medici art collections. Throughout the years, Medici descendants added works by Peter Paul Reubens, Titian, and others to the family collection. While the works of these artists can be seen in museums around the world, the largest number of them are located at the Uffizi Gallery in Florence. Upon her death, Ana Luisa, the last of the Medici line, asked that the collection stay in Florence. Her descendants opened the Uffizi to the public as a gallery in the 1760s, and it can still be visited to this day.

◄◄ Lorenzo's Legacy ►►

Lorenzo's art patronage helped to expand the Renaissance and led to scientific and academic advancements that changed the world forever.

WHEN LORENZO RULED...

Machu Picchu was being built in the Andes Mountains

Johannes Gutenberg introduced his printing press in Germany

Christopher Columbus arrived in the Caribbean

SÜLEYMAN THE MAGNIFICENT

THE SPLENDID SULTAN
(OTTOMAN EMPIRE, PRESENT-DAY TURKEY)

REIGN: 1520–1566

FATHER: Selim I / **MOTHER:** Hafsa Hatun

SUCCESSOR: Selim II

OTHER NAMES: Süleyman the Lawgiver, Süleyman the Just,
the Grand Turk, the Imperial Divan

WHAT WAS SO GREAT ABOUT SÜLEYMAN?

Süleyman is said to have brought a Golden Age to the Ottoman Empire. During his reign, the arts flourished and laws became more just. Süleyman made Constantinople (now Istanbul) the greatest city in the world during his time.

TOUGH BEGINNINGS

Süleyman's father, Selim, was actually called Selim the Terrible, in part because he had gone to war with his own father to gain the throne. Selim killed his brothers, his nephews, and all of his sons except Süleyman. He *tried* to murder Süleyman by sending him a poisoned shirt. But Süleyman's page tried it on first and died instantly (unlucky for him and lucky for Süleyman). Needless to say, Süleyman had a lot to overcome in his early years.

As a young man, Süleyman followed the tradition of all the sultans—he learned a trade. He chose gold smithing, and that eventually led to his lifelong support of the arts (see page 68) and learning.

MAGNIFICENT TIMES

Like the sultans before him, Süleyman spent much of his early reign expanding his empire. His court at Topkapi Palace was considered the most educated in the world at the time. It was a hot spot for the top artists and thinkers. Craft guilds (see below) began to thrive. Literacy within his empire expanded (for some, at least). Constantinople (the original name of Istanbul) was an exciting and diverse city. Greeks, Bulgarians, Serbians, Armenians, Jews, Russians, and Poles flocked to the city for opportunities in education and trade during Süleyman's years as ruler.

Those who knew him found Süleyman charming, well read, and intelligent. He spoke five languages and was reported to be a good conversationalist. When an ambassador from Venice arrived at Süleyman's court, he said, "The Turkish Court is

BY ORDER OF THE SULTAN

— — — — — — —

Süleyman's empire was vast. From one end to the other, there were dozens of different cultures. While there were many cities within his territory, there were also remote outposts that didn't have a lot of contact with the rest of the empire. To make sure that *all* the people of his empire were treated fairly, Süleyman updated the laws and made an effort to ensure they were all enforced fairly and consistently. He did this by appointing local officials who answered to a higher-ranking member of his court. This replaced the previous system, in which local officials weren't held accountable to anyone. The rights of the empire's religious minorities—such as the Christians and Jews—were protected under his reign. Instead of leaving punishment up to local authorities, specific fines were set and enforced throughout the empire. Corruption was taken seriously, and corrupt officials had their lands and goods confiscated. Süleyman also freed captives from previous wars.

Süleyman believed that a more just society was better for his empire. Long after he died, his rules stayed in place, and Süleyman became known as "Süleyman the Just" and "Süleyman the Lawmaker."

a superb sight, and most superb is the Sultan himself. One's eyes are dazzled by the gleam of gold and jewelry. Silk and brocade shimmer in flashing rays. What strikes one about Süleyman the Magnificent is not his flowing robes or his high turban. He is unique among the throng because his demeanor is that of a truly great emperor."

But historians say that one of Süleyman's greatest strengths was something that still makes a good leader today: he had a knack for recognizing and hiring the best people and letting them shine without micromanaging them. An Austrian ambassador said of him: "In making his appointments, the Sultan pays no regard to any pretensions on the score of wealth or rank, nor does he take into consideration recommendations or popularity; he considers each case on its own merits, and examines carefully the character, ability and disposition of the man whose promotion is in question." In the past, it had been hard for anyone to get a job without money or family connections. Hiring people based on their ability instead of their connections produced great results for Süleyman: the empire operated smoothly during his reign.

ARTISTIC OTTOMANS

Because he had been trained as a goldsmith, Süleyman appreciated the importance of the arts. He wanted artistic expression to thrive in his empire. He encouraged what he called "communities of the talented"—the Ottoman equivalent of the guilds that existed in parts of Europe. Süleyman developed workshops at his palaces so that artists and craftspeople had a place to work. These artists included rug weavers, metalsmiths, book binders, jewelers, woodworkers, and many more types of craftspeople. They came from all over the empire and brought their own artistic styles with them. Süleyman displayed their works in his palaces.

The communities of the talented had an apprenticeship system and were well paid once they became professional craftspeople. Süleyman didn't believe in the idea of starving artists!

CREATING CONSTANTINOPLE

Süleyman wanted Constantinople to be world-class. So he set out to make sure the city's architecture was unforgettable. To do that, he hired the best architect he could find—a man named Sinan.

As the empire's official architect, Sinan had the job of making Istanbul and other Ottoman cities look impressive. In particular, Süleyman wanted his empire to seem just as important as, if not more important than, the early Byzantine (or late Roman) empire. Part of this plan was to create a mosque that was as breathtaking as the Hagia Sophia, a Byzantine church that was the largest building in the world at that time.

Sinan had spent many years as a soldier in the Ottoman army and traveled around the empire—visiting Egypt, Persia, and many other places. He took the opportunity to study the architecture of bygone civilizations as he traveled. "I saw the great ancient remains. From every ruin I learned, from every building I absorbed something," he wrote.

Sinan used what he knew to help design the Süleymaniye Mosque (Süleyman's Mosque), which was situated on a hill dominating the city of Constantinople. He had a big job to consider. In addition to making the mosque graceful, beautiful, and spiritual, it had to be strong enough to withstand earthquakes. He surrounded the mosque with schools, a hospital, library, bookshops, and public baths. Nearly five hundred years and several earthquakes later, the mosque complex is still standing.

Sinan's success inspired many other architects, and Constantinople experienced a building boom that helped make it one of the world's greatest cities. But Sinan also designed incredible buildings elsewhere in the empire, including the Dome of the Rock in Jerusalem and the Kaaba in Mecca. All in all, Sinan directed over three hundred projects in his lifetime.

A LOVER, NOT A FIGHTER

In addition to ruling over a large portion of the world, Süleyman also wrote poetry under the pen name Muhhibi, which means "lover." Although he wrote poems on a lot of topics, he really did prefer writing about love. He would even write love poems to his wife while on the battlefield. *My delight, my wine, my orange my candle of night, my sugar, my treasure*—he had a lot of very romantic things to say to her. Süleyman's poetry still exists today, and many claim it's still the greatest in the entire Islamic world.

◄◄ Süleyman's Legacy ►►

Süleyman's reform of the laws helped keep the Ottoman Empire together for over three hundred years. The great buildings he commissioned, such as the Süleymaniye Mosque, are still some of the world's most impressive structures, nearly five hundred years after his rule.

WHEN SÜLEYMAN WAS SULTAN...

the potato was introduced to Europe (from South America)

Europeans set foot in Japan for the first time

the first enslaved people were brought to Brazil from West Africa

NUR JAHAN

THE QUEEN OF QUEENS (INDIA)

REIGN: 1611–1627

FATHER: Mirza Ghiyas Beg / **MOTHER:** Asmat Begum

SUCCESSOR: Shah Jahan

OTHER NAMES: Nur Mahal (Light of the Palace),
Padshah Begam (Imperial Lady)

. . .

WHAT WAS SO GREAT ABOUT NUR JAHAN?

While other women had played important roles in Indian history, Nur Jahan was the first co-ruler, influencing not just cultural life but also government. She worked tirelessly on all fronts—from trade to social services and the arts—leaving a mark that's still felt today in India.

GREAT BEGINNINGS

Born to Persian parents who immigrated to India, Mehrunnisa (who would later be known as Nur Jahan) grew up at the court of Akbar the Great. Her father worked his way up to a position similar to that of a modern-day prime minister. As a child, Mehrunnisa wrote poetry and learned to love art, music, and dancing. She married a government official and moved to Bengal, where it's said she learned to hunt tigers. She and her husband had one child, a daughter named Ladili. But Mehrunnisa's husband was killed under mysterious circumstances. She became a widow at age thirty and was sent to the court of the Mughal emperor to become a lady-in-waiting. That's when her future changed forever.

LEGENDARY FASHION SENSE

Nur Jahan was known for her beauty but also for her personal style. She wore her clothes sewn instead of wrapped around the body as Indian women had done until that time. She is known as the inventor of the Punjabi style of women's clothing, which is still worn today.

She was also a textile designer. Nur Jahan loved embroidery and often did it in her spare time. She helped develop new kinds of lightweight fabrics that would be easier for women to wear in hot weather and designed floral patterns for them. She introduced the idea of adding silver threads to fabrics to make them more special.

The Lady Emperor also loved cosmetics, especially perfume. She developed her own signature rose-based scent. It was said to be so strong, a single drop would last for eight months.

Nur Jahan designed a type of inexpensive wedding clothes that even poor couples could afford for their special day. Today's wedding fashions in India are still inspired by her designs.

Nur Jahan even made garments for the imperial elephants, embroidered "caparisons" (a kind of saddle) made from recycled mailbags.

POWER COUPLE

The story goes that Emperor Jahangir (son of Akbar the Great) saw Mehrunnisa and fell instantly and deeply in love with her. He asked her to marry him and she accepted, becoming somewhere between his twelfth and twentieth wife. Once they were married, he began calling her Nur Jahan (meaning "Light of the World").

As a lesser wife to the emperor, Nur Jahan wasn't supposed to be remarkable. But her brilliance couldn't be contained. Jahangir consulted her on all decisions. Eventually, he let her take over duties that he wasn't interested in, such as meetings with visiting trade ambassadors. Her head appeared on coins next to her husband's. She signed orders as "the Lady Emperor." A Dutch visitor to the court once said that Nur Jahan actually made *all* the decisions involved in ruling the country and

Jahangir was emperor in name only. Jahangir is reported to have said, "My wife has wit enough in her little finger to rule the whole kingdom without my troubling my head about it. All I need is a bottle of wine and piece of meat to keep myself merry." (In fact, he is thought to have had entirely too much wine—and opium—by this point in his life.)

A MULTITALENTED MONARCH

There was seemingly nothing Nur Jahan wasn't good at. When she heard of a problem, she could solve it immediately and effectively. She was witty and charming. Her empire was at the center of the world's spice, jewel, and cloth trades. She was in charge of deciding what goods could come into and go out of her kingdom, collecting taxes, and granting approval for foreign merchants to do business in the Mughal Empire.

Nur Jahan also supported the arts, including visual arts, architecture, music, and poetry. A poet herself, she could compose a verse on the spot. She sponsored poetry contests for women poets at her court and was the patron for several women poets of the time.

Nur Jahan engaged in a lot of what we would now call landscape design and city planning. She designed public gardens, with fountains, fruit trees, and even a manmade waterfall lit from behind with hundreds of lamps. When her beloved parents died, she designed their tombs, which are said to have inspired the Taj Mahal (later built for her niece [known as Mumtaz Mahal] by her stepson Shah Khurrum).

Nur Jahan showed great care for the poor, too. In her time, it was impossible for a girl to get married without a dowry (some kind of money or goods her parents could offer to the parents of her intended husband). Nur Jahan provided dowries for around 500 poor girls so they could be married (unmarried women had few rights and protections back then).

One of the best-known stories about Nur Jahan is how she shot four tigers with six bullets, all while sitting on top of an elephant. This story was recorded by Jahangir, who noted that elephants move around a lot when they smell tigers, making Nur

Jahan's marksmanship even more impressive. There are other stories of her leading armies from atop an elephant and saving a servant by pulling an arrow from her arm and stopping the bleeding. Nur Jahan was said to have been injured once while riding an injured elephant, but she somehow survived. There's another story that she shot a man-eating tiger with a musket. Eventually, people started calling her "Tiger Slayer."

FAMILY DRAMA

No royal family is complete without a little drama, and the Moghul emperors were no exception. Nur Jahan got along well with her stepsons—that is, until she chose the younger one to marry her daughter, Ladili. This didn't sit well with the oldest son, Shah Khurrum. When Emperor Jahangir died, Shah Khurrum raised a force against his younger brother and killed him to make sure he didn't inherit the throne. Threatened by Nur Jahan's lasting power, he exiled her to Lahore (then another city in the Mughal Empire, but currently in Pakistan). There, she lived a quiet life with her daughter, Ladili, who was also now a widow. She continued to help the poor up until the time of her death in 1645.

WARRIOR QUEENS

• • • • • • • • •

While Nur Jahan's tiger-slaying reputation was legendary, she's just one of many Indian queens known for bravery. Razia Sultana (1236–1240) was the first woman to rule over both a major empire and an Islamic country. She was known as a just ruler and a warrior. Abbakka Chowta (1525–1570), known as The Fearless, fought the Portuguese to maintain control of her kingdom. Queen Ahilyabai Holkar (1725–1795) acted as general, leading warriors into battle against invaders from two neighboring kingdoms. The best known of the warrior queens, however, is the Rani of Jhansi (1828–1858), who led a rebellion against the British and is known as "the Joan of Arc of India."

AT HER MAJESTY'S TABLE

Nur Jahan was said to be a wonderful hostess. She loved entertaining and was very involved in court parties and dinners. Having grown up eating Persian food, she is said to have introduced elements of it to India, including candied fruit peels and red wine mixed with sherbet, which was a refreshing beverage.

When she entertained, Nur Jahan paid attention to the presentation of the food. Color and fragrance were added to foods so that they satisfied all the senses.

 Nur Jahan's Legacy

The public spaces Nur Jahan designed are still in use today and her aesthetic has influenced Indian art for centuries. Her sense of style and entertaining still influences Indian culture today, too.

WHEN NUR JAHAN WAS QUEEN...

witch hunts were happening all over Europe

the Puritans were settling New England

Galileo was speaking out on his theories about the solar system

GOOD QUEEN BESS (ELIZABETH I)

ENGLAND'S ETERNAL QUEEN

REIGN: 1558–1603

FATHER: Henry VIII / **MOTHER:** Anne Boleyn

HALF SIBLINGS: Mary Tudor and Edward VI

SUCCESSOR: James VI

OTHER NAMES: Gloriana, the Virgin Queen

...

WHAT WAS SO GREAT ABOUT ELIZABETH?

Elizabeth inherited a very difficult situation when she came to the throne—her country had been torn apart by religious and political conflict for years. She restored relative peace and order while on the throne. With things running more smoothly at home, she was able to set her sights on the rest of the world. She sponsored explorers, positioned England as a world superpower, and helped English culture to develop and thrive.

AN UNHAPPY FAMILY

Elizabeth's father, King Henry VIII, really wanted a son. Really, *really* badly. So badly that when he realized he and his first wife, Catherine, would only have a daughter together (Mary, see page 119), he started a whole new religion so he could divorce Catherine and marry someone else to try for a son.

Henry's second wife was Elizabeth's mother: Anne Boleyn. When Elizabeth was born, Henry was disappointed. He longed for a son, and when he didn't get one, he had Anne's head chopped off (Elizabeth was just three years old.) Henry married

another woman, Jane. Jane did give him a son (thankfully for her). Now, Elizabeth had a half brother, Edward, who was four years younger than she was. The three half siblings—Mary, Elizabeth, and Edward—all lived in different palaces and didn't see each other much. Elizabeth was raised mostly by her nanny and rarely saw her father, the king. She was only thirteen years old when he died, and Edward—only nine years old—became king. Elizabeth never expected to become queen.

IT'S COMPLICATED

Edward did not rule for long. He died at the age of fifteen. Upon his death, Elizabeth's older half sister, Mary, became queen. Things then became even more complicated for the royal sisters. Mary had Elizabeth thrown into jail in the Tower of London for plotting to overthrow her (she hadn't). Mary even ordered Elizabeth to be executed. But Elizabeth was eventually released. A few years later, the sisters made up and Mary decided Elizabeth could be her heir. Mary died at age forty-two, and Elizabeth became queen at age twenty-five.

GOOD WORK

Elizabeth was a very practical queen. She knew that in order to get anything done, she'd have to stop all the fighting about religion in her country. Soon after she became queen, Elizabeth passed several acts that helped bring an end to the religious power struggle (at least temporarily).

She also knew that the country had to stop overspending and to bring in more revenue (income). Elizabeth decided to get a better handle on England's budget. She increased revenue through trade and established The Royal Exchange, a kind of early stock exchange. (Unfortunately, some of that revenue was made through stealing from the Spanish and through the slave trade.)

Elizabeth helped start the Age of Exploration while she was queen. With her backing, Sir Francis Drake circumnavigated the globe—once in a single expedition. In her time, Sir Walter Raleigh and others set out to map and explore the world. This set the stage for the expansion of the British Empire that began after her death.

AT HER MAJESTY'S COURT

When Elizabeth became queen, she inherited over sixty royal residences! If it sounds like a lot of homes to take care of, it was. (Many were in a bad state at the beginning of her reign, and more fell down over the course of it.)

Elizabeth and her court of up to around a thousand people would move from palace to palace every few weeks. Some of her favorite dwellings were Whitehall, Hampton Court, Richmond, and Windsor. She liked to spend Christmas at Whitehall, for example, and Easter at Windsor.

Elizabeth hosted foreign ambassadors and other visitors at her court. During the day, she'd meet with advisors, then walk, ride, hunt, or sometimes hawk with members of the court. At night, lavish banquets were held with five courses, including dishes such as boar, venison, and sturgeon. After dinner, there would be music, dancing, and theater productions.

So many people living in once place at one time meant the palaces were very "lived in" (read: smelly and dirty) and had to be aired out every few weeks. The empty palace had to be cleaned and made ready for another royal visit at any moment. Elizabeth's favorite palaces were so well cared for that you can still visit them today.

During Elizabeth's reign, the arts flourished, especially drama and literature. She encouraged and supported playwrights and poets, including, most famously, William Shakespeare. Works written during the Elizabethan period are still considered some of the most important works in English literature.

But perhaps what Elizabeth is best known for is defeating the Spanish Armada, a fleet sent to destroy England in 1588. Until then, Spain was the undisputed sea power of the world. Spain's control of the seas meant they had an advantage in everything from trade to exploration. But with this victory, England became a world superpower. Now England could develop its own trade relationships overseas, leading to colonization and the development of the empire.

Although her father didn't have any expectations for her, Elizabeth had become a much, much better ruler than either he or her siblings ever were. She was able to help England grow from a small island kingdom to an important player on the world stage.

FORSOOTH, DOEST THOU SAYEST? VERILY!

If you were able to travel back in time, would you be able to understand the English spoken in Elizabeth's England? There are several differences between the English spoken now and Elizabethan English, known as Early Modern English.

The period of Early Modern English describes a time when the pronunciation of vowels in English was starting to change. In Elizabeth's time, *tea* was pronounced "tay" and *hour* was pronounced "oar," for example. If you listened hard enough, though, you would probably be able to figure out what was being said.

There was also a lot of vocabulary at the time that you wouldn't know, but you might be able to guess. For example: What does "How dost thou?" sound like? If you guessed "How are you?" you'd be right. *Thee, thou,* and *thy* were still used instead of *you* and *your. Will* was *wilst; do* was *dost; why* was *wherefore;* and *are* was *art,* as in "Wherefore art thou, Romeo?"—Juliet's famous question.

Many new words in the language were introduced in this period, too. Experts say that Shakespeare himself added nearly two thousand words to the English language, including *puppy dog, alligator,* and *eyeball.* He also introduced many phrases, such as "dead as a doornail" and "breaking the ice," into the language.

The new Globe Theater in London now produces some of Shakespeare's plays in the original pronunciation from the Elizabethan Era.

THE OTHER MARY

Although Elizabeth had a difficult relationship with her half sister Mary, things with her *cousin* Mary were even rougher. Because she shared their religion, some powerful Catholic people thought that Elizabeth's cousin Mary Stuart, aka Mary Queen of Scots, should be queen instead of Elizabeth. Mary asked that Elizabeth name her as her heir. Elizabeth said that she didn't want to name *anyone* as her heir—she had seen what had happened in her parents' time and thought that was just asking for trouble. A lot of drama took place between the cousins over the course of many years. Mary was forced to abdicate her throne in Scotland to her half brother and came to England to seek Elizabeth's help in getting it back. She got wrapped up in a plot to have Elizabeth overthrown. Elizabeth put Mary under house arrest. Then Elizabeth's advisors had Mary's head chopped off, possibly without Elizabeth's knowledge. It was a sad end to a very unhappy family feud.

Elizabeth's Legacy

The stability Elizabeth brought to England didn't last, but she did help move her country toward becoming the global superpower it was during the reign of the next woman to take the throne: Queen Victoria (1819–1901).

WHEN ELIZABETH WAS QUEEN...

Ivan the Terrible (see page 125) was tsar of Russia

the Incan Empire fell completely to Spain

the colony of Roanoke (in what's now North Carolina) was founded and its colonists later mysteriously disappeared

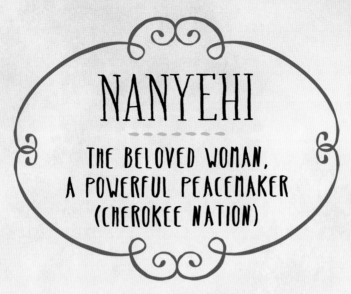

NANYEHI

THE BELOVED WOMAN, A POWERFUL PEACEMAKER (CHEROKEE NATION)

REIGN: 1755–1785

MOTHER: Tame Doe / **FATHER (POSSIBLY):** Fivekiller

OTHER NAMES: Nancy Ward, Tsistunagiska ("Wild Rose")

• • •

WHAT WAS SO GREAT ABOUT NANYEHI?

Nanyehi lived during a very difficult time in Cherokee history. Her nation was trying to preserve its culture and keep its territory while learning to live side by side with new neighbors—the European Americans. Through times of great conflict, she was a peacemaker who tried to help both cultures coexist.

A CHEROKEE CHILDHOOD

Nanyehi was born around 1738 as a member of the Wolf Clan, one of the seven Cherokee clans that lived in the Southeast. At that time, the Cherokee were just starting to recover from a smallpox epidemic that had killed about a third of their nation's population. Nanyehi lived in the town of Chota in what's now eastern Tennessee. Her uncle was the chief, Attakullakulla, who had traveled to England, lived there for four months, met King George II, and signed agreements for trade and British settlement on Cherokee land.

Like most Cherokee women, Nanyehi married young and had children. She lived an ordinary life until the day she accompanied her husband, Kingfisher, into battle.

BECOMING BELOVED

In 1755, Nanyehi (just eighteen years old) went along with her husband and a war party as they went to battle with the Creeks in Georgia. As the battle raged, it's said that Nanyehi helped by chewing on bullets to make them sharper and more lethal. When her husband was killed, Nanyehi took his place in the fight, jumping out from behind a tree and rallying the troops. In recognition of her bravery, she was given the title Ghigau (pronounced GIG-a-who), which means both "Beloved Woman" and "War Woman." This was the highest honor a Cherokee woman could receive, given to those who defended Cherokee warriors. As Ghigau, Nanyehi had a vote in council affairs, could negotiate treaties, and was given the special right of deciding whether or not a prisoner would be saved from execution.

CHEROKEE WOMEN

Cherokee women had many more rights than women in the culture that eventually took over their lands. The women owned land and dwellings. When they wanted a divorce, they could just place their husband's things outside the door, and he'd have to find another place to live.

While duties were divided by gender (men hunted; women tended the fields), equal value was put on both kinds of work. Women were considered the head of the household. Women owned the home buildings and passed them down to their daughters. Their voices were equal in votes about important clan matters.

When the Cherokee began negotiating with the British, they were surprised that no women were in attendance on behalf of the British. "You were born of women just as we were, were you not? Why do you not take them into your council?" a Cherokee chief is reported to have asked. As the Cherokee adopted more American principles and laws, though, women were given less say. In 1827, a Cherokee woman's right to vote was taken away in order to be more in line with laws of the US government.

TURBULENT TIMES

During Nanyehi's life, her people were almost constantly at war on all fronts. As settlers from the English colonies started to move farther west into Cherokee lands, there were frequent disputes. The Cherokee made some agreements with the British and more or less sided with them against the French, who owned land to the north and west of their territory.

At the same time, the Cherokee had disputes with other indigenous nations in the South. As the American colonists started to rebel against British rule, the British encouraged the Cherokee to attack colonial rebels. Some Cherokee sided with the

THE BITTER END

A s Nanyehi had wished, the Cherokee tried to live peacefully with the settlers. But times changed. Americans wanted the Cherokee to adopt their ways of life. They also wanted more Cherokee land. Some Cherokee, including Nanyehi, agreed that there were many parts of the new Americans' way of life that they were willing to adopt. Some converted to Christianity. Some learned to speak, read, and write English. A written Cherokee language was also developed by Sequoyah (a man from a prominent Cherokee family). Sequoyah thought that if the Cherokee could record their laws and stories in their own language, they would be in a better position of strength in relation to the American government.

But all the efforts of the Cherokee to try to maintain their status as an independent nation came to an end in 1830 when President Andrew Jackson signed the Indian Removal Act. This law was the first step in forcibly taking land from the indigenous nations east of the Mississippi. In 1838, members of the Cherokee nation were driven from their homeland and pushed west by federal forces on what came to be known as the Trail of Tears. Thousands of Cherokee died—of disease, cold, hunger, or murder—on this forced march.

British, while some (like Nanyehi) sided with those who would become known as the American patriots.

In such confusing times, Nanyehi always looked for the best path toward peace for her people. She believed that learning to live and work with the settlers was the best way. The leaders of new settlements would come to her when they had something to discuss with the Cherokee. A Spanish explorer named Solis described her this way: "There is an Indian woman of great authority and following whom they call . . . 'great lady.' Her house is very large and has many rooms. The rest of the nation brings presents and gifts to her. She has many Indian men and women in her service, and these are like priests and captains among them."

Nanyehi was known for advocating for freedom for settlers who had been taken prisoner. She famously used this right to save the life of a settler woman who had been captured. The two became friends. The settler, whose name was Lydia Bean, taught Nanyehi how to spin yarn, stich clothing, and make dairy products. The Cherokee, who had never raised cattle or used dairy before, added these practices to their way of farming. The friendship between Lydia and Nanyehi had an unintended long-term impact on the Cherokee way of life. As Cherokee adopted more of the settlers' ways, the imbalance of power between men and women grew. Cherokee women were soon required to tend the animals, so they were less involved in political decisions (see page 85).

As the Americans began fighting the Revolutionary War against England, Nanyehi heard that her cousin Dragging Canoe was planning an attack on an American settlement. She warned the Americans of the attack so they could be prepared. For this, she was recognized as a Daughter of the American Revolution.

In Cherokee culture, marriage was often short term. Since her first husband died, Nanyehi married a settler named Bryant Ward, who said that she was "the most superior woman I have ever met." The couple had a daughter named Elizabeth (nicknamed Betsy). It was at this time that Nanyehi became known as Nancy Ward, a name that stuck with her for the rest of her life.

Nanyehi's position on the clan council allowed her to be present at important negotiations between the Cherokee and the settlers. In one meeting in 1781, she made a strong case for peace. The US Army commissioner is said to have been so moved by her words that he promised that the settlers would remain peaceful if the Cherokee would, making no further demands for their land (this promise was later broken).

In her later years, Nanyehi wasn't as strong as she used to be, so when there were important meetings, she sent a messenger carrying both her message and her walking cane instead of going herself. She asked council leaders not to give away any more land to the Americans. But the land where she grew up was eventually sold and she had to move farther south. The US government continued to break treaties and refused to stop settlers from illegally taking more Cherokee land, despite all the agreements they came to with the Cherokee.

Nanyehi, now an old woman, opened an inn for travelers in what's now Tennessee. People began calling her "Granny Ward" because she took in and cared for orphans. She died around 1819.

◀◀ Nanyehi's Legacy ▶▶

Nanyehi is still remembered as one of the most memorable women in Cherokee history. Today, there are fewer than five living Cherokee people with the title Beloved Woman or Beloved Man.

WHEN NANYEHI WAS RULER...

the Revolutionary War was fought and won by the Americans

Shaka Zulu rose to power in Zululand (part of what's now South Africa)

the British were expanding their territory in India

KAMEHAMEHA the GREAT

HAWAI'I'S BIG KAHUNA

REIGN: circa 1782–1819

FATHER: Keoua Nui (Keoua the Great) /
MOTHER: Kekuiapoiwa

SUCCESSOR: Liholiho

OTHER NAMES: Pai'ea (birth name,
which means "hard shell crab"),
the Napoleon of the Pacific

• • •

WHAT WAS SO GREAT ABOUT KAMEHAMEHA?

Before Kamehameha, each of the islands of Hawai'i had its own ruler, and there was a lot of fighting among them. Kamehameha united the islands and led them through a difficult time in their history. He restored peace and helped Hawaiians to see themselves as one people—as part of the Kingdom of Hawai'i.

GREAT BEGINNINGS

Before Kamehameha was born, there was a prophecy on the island of Hawai'i that a great leader would soon be born (see page 92). So when a baby boy was born to the ruling family, he was hidden away in a valley to keep him from harm. (This might have been why he was given the name Kamehameha, which means "the Lonely One" or "the One Set Apart.") During his early years, Kamehameha learned war arts, sports, storytelling, seafaring, and navigation skills. It was said that he was an especially strong swimmer. He also grew very, very tall—some say he was seven feet by the time he reached adulthood!

ROCK AND RULE

Many cultures around the world seem to have a story that involves a rock with the magical power used to determine who should be the next leader of the kingdom (King Arthur and the sword in the stone is one example). In Hawaiian culture, the Naha stone was such a rock. When a boy of the Naha royal line was born, he was placed upon the stone with all the high priests in attendance. If the baby cried while on the stone, he would become a commoner. If he didn't, he was eligible to become king. Legend said that the man who could move the stone (estimated to weigh about 5,000 pounds) would unite the various islands and become king over all of Hawai'i.

According to one story, high priests and royals assembled to watch fourteen-year-old Kamehameha move the stone. It was said that his effort was so strong that the earth trembled and some thought there had been an earthquake. And he was successful. Everyone celebrated, and he became king. The story of Kamehameha's feat of strength spread throughout the islands, and some say that it helped secure his reputation as a fierce warrior as he went into battle.

Today, the Naha stone is located in front of the public library in Hilo, Hawai'i, so you can try moving it yourself!

A UNITED KINGDOM

The islands of Hawai'i were in a time of great conflict. As a young adult, Kamehameha fought in many battles. His reputation for fierceness and bravery spread throughout the islands.

BORN UNDER A GOOD SIGN

K amehameha's birth is shrouded in legend and mystery. It's said that there was a prophecy that when a light appeared in the sky with feathers like a bird, a great leader would be born. Kamehameha is thought to have been born in 1758, the year Halley's Comet was visible from Hawai'i.

(Kamehameha isn't the only legendary leader whose birth is said to have been predicted by the stars. The births of Jesus as well as the Roman emperor Julius Caesar and Alexander the Great were also said to have been foretold by great, bright-shining stars.)

Not only was he a skilled warrior, but Kamehameha was good at strategy. By using his trading skills, he developed a big supply of weapons from the British and Americans. They not only sold weapons to him, but they showed him how to use them. Kamehameha even commissioned some English carpenters to build a big war ship for him. Two British soldiers became Kamehameha's close advisors.

One by one, Kamehameha conquered the Hawaiian Islands, starting with his own island of Hawai'i and moving on to other islands, gaining power through a combination of battles and peaceful agreements with local rulers. His success as a warrior didn't happen overnight, though. It took more than a decade for Kamehameha to become the sole ruler of the islands of Hawai'i. Being persistent was one of Kamehameha's strengths.

Kamehameha was a good businessman, too. During his life, big trading ships were crossing the Pacific from the Americas to China. The fur trade had decreased by this time, and traders were looking for a popular new product. They hit upon sandalwood (from a kind of tree that grows in Hawai'i). It was good for building and making incense and perfume. Kamehameha developed a sandalwood monopoly and got a big percentage of the profit from every shipment that left his shores.

AMERICA'S REAL ROYAL FAMILY

- - - - - - - -

People refer to celebrity families as "America's royal family." But there has really been only one royal family on American soil: Kamehameha's family, the Royal House of Kawānanakoa.

Because Hawai'i didn't have a single, central government before Kamehameha took power, he became the first true king of Hawai'i. The next four leaders after him also used the name Kamehameha. Kamehameha V has been described as the last great traditional ruler of Hawai'i. Although he followed a traditional style of leadership, he was very modern for his time. He traveled all over the Americas in his youth. He hosted foreign dignitaries, including monarchs and well-known people, such as Mark Twain. When he died, his cousin Lunalilo became king. He was called "the People's King" because he had been elected by popular vote. He made a lot of democratic reforms in Hawai'i. His wife, Queen Emma, was a powerful figure, too, and became the lifelong friend of Queen Victoria, who she visited in England.

King David Kalakaua (known as the Merry Monarch) took over next. During his reign, Hawai'i became a constitutional monarchy like the United Kingdom. King David was known for playing the ukulele and songwriting, surfing, and reviving hula dancing. He built Iolani Palace, inspired by royal palaces he had seen in his travels throughout Europe. When he died, his sister Lili'uokalani became queen. She was a famous songwriter, who was later placed under house arrest when powerful foreigners took over Hawai'i. She was the last queen of Hawai'i.

Lili'uokalani's niece, Princess Kaiulani, worked to try to get the royal family restored to the throne. While she became known internationally—both for her intelligence and her beauty—she was not successful in her efforts.

Today, Hawai'i's "last princess"—Abigail Kinoiki Kekaulike Kawānanakoa—is in her nineties. She is Lili'uokalani's great-grandniece and the last true royal on American ground.

He also taxed ships that docked in his harbor. He made a fortune and used it to help develop the islands.

Kamehameha's main accomplishment, though, was keeping his people free from the rule of the British, Americans, and Russians. Although Hawai'i later became a US state, the independence it established under Kamehameha's rule helped preserve Hawaiian culture so that it wasn't lost even after Hawai'i became part of the United States.

Kamehameha's Legacy

In Hawai'i, June 11 is celebrated as Kamehameha Day. There is a floral parade in Honolulu that ends at Iolani Palace. Kamehameha's statue located there is adorned with a lei (flower wreath). He is still considered the father of Hawai'i.

WHEN KAMEHAMEHA WAS KING...

steam transportation was developed

Beethoven's "Fifth Symphony" was written

the slave trade was outlawed in Britain

the empire-waist dress came into fashion

HALL of WORTHIES

There are so many more great rulers throughout history that
it's worth noting a few of them here.

Akbar the Great (India: 1556–1605)

The third Mughal emperor, Akbar promoted peace and education,
improved the economy, and was a supporter of the arts and culture.

Catherine the Great (Russia: 1762–1796)

The first Russian empress, Catherine improved education and health
care in her country while amassing a world-class art collection.

Charles the Great, aka Charlemagne (France: 768–814)

The first great leader after the fall of the Roman Empire, Charlemagne
united Europe and sparked a new interest in learning and culture.

Huayna Capac, the Mighty One (Inca: 1493–1524)

Known as a great warrior, Huayna Capac also expanded the Incan
Empire and built temples and roads.

Naresuan the Great (Thailand and Myanmar: 1590–1605)

Naresuan is known primarily for his bravery and the elephant battle, in
which he challenged another king to a duel atop an elephant—
and won.

Ramses the Great (Egypt: 1292–1190 BCE)

Considered the greatest pharaoh of the Old Kingdom, Ramses was
known for his military might and for the temples and monuments he
had built during his reign.

Sargon the Great (Mesopotamia: 2334–2284 BCE)

Sargon (like the Bible's Moses) is said to have been placed in a basket in the river by his mother to be saved from death. He was then found and raised by a king. He's known for building a great empire and for inventing the idea of sending letters as a means of communication.

Sayyida al Hurra, the Honored (Morocco: 1515–1542)

A Moroccan queen, Sayyida al Hurra was forced to flee her kingdom and joined forces with a legendary pirate, then later married a king. She was known for ruling the seas along the coast of Morocco and helping her people maintain independence.

Taksin the Great (Thailand: 1767–1782)

Taksin is best known for promoting diplomacy and trade, building infrastructure, restoring temples, and promoting the arts.

Tamar the Great (Georgia: 1184–1213)

Tamar served as the first female king of the country, uniting and expanding her empire and leading to a golden age of culture for her people.

Toregene, the Great Khatun (Mongol Empire: 1241–1246)

Toregene ruled the Mongol Empire for five years, encouraging good relations with China and serving as a strong administrator.

Yu the Great (China: 2123–2025 BCE)

Described in some of the oldest records of China, Yu is known as "He Who Controls the Waters" for introducing flood control to the country.

THE
TERRIBLES

ATTILA THE HUN

THE SCOURGE OF GOD, ONE OF HISTORY'S MOST HATED (HUN EMPIRE, PRESENT-DAY CENTRAL ASIA AND EASTERN EUROPE)

REIGN: 434–453 CE

FATHER: Mundzuk / **MOTHER:** Unknown

SIBLINGS: Bleda

SUCCESSORS: Ellac, Dengizich, and Emak (his sons)

OTHER NAMES: Little Father, Hammer of the World

• • •

WHAT WAS SO TERRIBLE ABOUT ATTILA?

Attila is said to have liked his Latin nickname *Flagellum Dei,* which translates to "Scourge of God" or "God's Punishment." For much of his life, Attila's job was to keep the Romans on the run. Since the Romans wrote much of the Western history we know, it's no surprise he gained such a bad reputation.

GRAZIA, ATTILA!

While Attila sacked many ancient Roman cities in Italy, his looting and plundering was actually responsible for the development of one of the most beautiful cities in the world: Venice. As local people fled from the Huns, they crossed marshy areas on the Venetian lagoon and hid out on islands there. Soon buildings began to be erected in this part of the country, later becoming the now-famous city full of canals and winding side streets.

WHO WERE THE HUNS?

At its peak, Attila's empire spanned from modern-day Netherlands to Hungary. Through the years, the Huns sacked hundreds of cities in Greece, France, and Italy. Their military campaigns reached the outskirts of Paris, Constantinople, and Rome itself.

Unlike the super-organized Roman armies, the Huns were known for their swift and mighty surprise attacks from all directions. Opponents didn't know how

ATTILA THE HUN: FACT OR FICTION?

- - - - - - -

Notorious figures are often the subjects of stories, true and false. Lots of stories have developed around Attila. But are they true? Here are some of the most common tales and rumors about the Hun leader:

Attila had his brother murdered.
Probably false

This is a very popular story. While fratricide is a common theme among rulers both good and bad (see pages 43 and 137), there's not much proof that Attila murdered his brother, Bleda.

Attila died of a nosebleed on his wedding night.
Maybe true

After suffering his worst defeat, Attila returned to his home base in modern-day Hungary and married a woman named Ildico. At the wedding, he is said to have had too much to drink. The next morning he was found dead, with blood running out of his nose. It had also run into his mouth, possibly choking him. Although Attila's body has never been found (see page 105), experts believe that he likely suffered a brain

to defend themselves from the stealthy Huns. Hun warriors were said to be one with their horses and were rumored to be taught to ride a horse as soon as they could walk.

When Hun boys were babies, their cheeks were slashed to improve their ability to withstand pain. The resulting scars made their faces "fearsome" to look at, said Roman historian Jordanes. The Romans believed this scarring ritual meant that the Huns were cruel to children, and this made them even more intimidating. One

hemorrhage. Through the years, some said he was murdered by his new bride. The only certain thing is that we'll never know for certain.

Attila was a good negotiator.

True

Attila may have loved making war, but he also might have just done it for the cash. After inflicting so much damage on their cities, the Romans started paying Attila to keep the peace. He kept upping the price every year, so while he wasn't always defeating the Romans in battle, he was helping to drain their treasuries.

Attila's conquest of Rome was stopped by St. Peter and St. Paul.

False

As Attila's army headed toward Rome, Pope Leo rode out to meet him at the Po River in northern Italy. The two had a discussion and Attila turned around and went home. That much is true, but the rest of the story is a little cloudy. Some say that St. Peter and St. Paul (who had already been dead for hundreds of years) accompanied the pope. Most likely that's due to the creative license of the painter Raphael, who painted the two saints into a scene of the meeting. Another explanation is that the plague may have weakened the Hun army, and Attila became convinced that they couldn't win. Another theory is that they had run out of food and supplies and wouldn't be able to make it to Rome anyway.

SWORD OF DESTINY

Like other legendary leaders (see pages 9 and 89), Attila has an interesting origin story. It's said that a Hun shepherd was out tending his sheep and saw that one of his flock had a wound. As he looked for the source, he found an amazing sword. He brought the sword to Attila, who believed it was the sword of Mars (the Roman god of war). Now that he had it, he would rule the entire world. Of course, he really became leader because his uncle, who was the Hun's leader, had died. But the sword story helped build his fierce reputation.

Roman historian described Attila and the Hun army as the children of witches and demons. They didn't even use fire or cook their food, one account said—they just put meat between their thighs and the sides of their horses and while riding, the meat was heated. Because the Huns didn't have a written language, the Roman accounts are among the only impressions we have of the Huns.

After Attila died, the Huns were defeated within a year and disappeared from Europe soon after.

ATTILA IN ACTION

While the Romans would conquer a city then move in and set up government, Attila had a "scorched earth" policy. He'd come in, take everything valuable, kill the people, and burn the city to the ground. He wasn't interested in spreading the Hun culture.

Attila maintained his strength through fear. Rather than collecting taxes, Attila received tributes from the Roman Empire. Tribute was money paid to Attila to keep him from attacking parts of the empire.

There are many stories about Attila's fearsome personality. "Where I have passed, the grass will never grow again," he is supposed to have said. Some reported that he had a terrible temper. Pictures of Attila made him out to have devil's horns and a little beard.

But others paint a different picture of the Hun leader. A Roman historian named Priscus who spent time with Attila's army said that he was really a humble man. While others used gold and silver plates and goblets, Attila's were made of wood. He never wore jewels or gold. He has also been described as generous, giving the booty he plundered to his soldiers instead of keeping it for himself.

German stories describe Attila as a good ally, and even his enemies tended to say he was a man of his word. In stories from Hungary and Turkey, he's described as a wise leader. Because Attila didn't leave any written records, we have to rely on accounts of him by others, and they all depend on who is telling the story.

THE MYSTERY OF ATTILA'S GRAVE

The location of Attila's grave is a mystery. After his death, his soldiers are said to have cut their cheeks with blades so that they would cry blood instead of tears, in order to appear more manly. They are said to have ridden their horses in circles around the tent where his body was being held, then had a series of coffins made (like nesting dolls, there was one inside another: first gold, then silver, then iron).

According to the story, the soldiers diverted a river and placed the coffins in the river bed so the water would later flow back over the coffins to hide them. After the burial was finished, those who had helped with it were killed so they could never reveal the location. Adventure seekers still try to find the grave, but so far, none have succeeded.

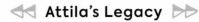

◀◀ Attila's Legacy ▶▶

Attila is best known for weakening the Roman Empire so that it crumbled not long after his time. (In truth, it had been in bad shape for some time, and he was just another blow to it.) Attila is remembered as a hero in Hungary, and, in fact, Attila is still a popular baby name for boys there today.

IF YOU HAD LIVED IN ATTILA'S TIME... YOU WOULD HAVE:

probably not have known how to read or write

learned to ride a horse by the time you were three years old

had parents who may have bound your head to give it a more conical shape, which was the fashion at the time

BAD KING JOHN

A LACKLUSTER LEGACY (ENGLAND)

REIGN: 1199–1216
FATHER: Henry II / **MOTHER:** Eleanor of Aquitaine
SUCCESSOR: Henry III
OTHER NAMES: John Lackland, John Softsword

• • •

WHAT WAS SO TERRIBLE ABOUT KING JOHN?

Suspicious. Treacherous. Greedy. Cowardly. Those are some of the *nicer* adjectives people used to describe King John during his reign. In fact, people today don't think much more of him. The British people recently voted King John one of the worst kings in English history and *the* worst person in the entire thirteenth century! John earned this reputation through his self-serving policies and cruelty to everyone around him.

BAD BLOOD

John was part of a family so bad that everyone called them "the Devil's Brood": the Plantagenet royal family, which started in France and came to rule over England and Scotland. John wasn't expected to become king. The youngest of five boys, he was said to have been a spoiled child. While his brothers were out learning jousting, he stuck to his favorite hobby: collecting jewelry. His father—King Henry II—gave all the good baronies and dukedoms to his older brothers so John got the nickname Lackland.

John's older brothers died, leaving only Richard the Lionheart (see page 110), who became king once their father died. As is obvious from his nickname, Richard was considered very brave. He went off to fight in the Crusades in the Holy Land. But when he was on his way back in 1192, he was captured and imprisoned by the king

of Austria. John saw this as an opportunity. If Richard stayed in prison, John would get to be king. So John bribed Richard's captor to keep his brother in jail.

Richard was eventually freed and heard of John's attempt at bribery. But he forgave John because "he was only a child" (he was twenty-seven). When Richard died in 1199, John started a war to prevent his nephew Arthur from getting the throne. Then Arthur conveniently "disappeared," leaving no more threats to John's position as king. He took up the throne months after Richard died.

BAD BEHAVIOR

John had a way of making enemies wherever he went. Before he became king, his father sent John to rule Ireland as a lord. But once there, John laughed at the local chiefs who came to greet him and pulled their beards (beards were really uncool

ROBIN HOOD AND KING JOHN: THE TRUE STORY

Robin Hood, the outlaw of Sherwood Forest, stole from the rich and gave to the poor. He constantly outsmarted Bad King John. That story has endured for centuries, but how true is it?

Some historians think *someone* named Robin Hood might have lived after the time of King John, and that his story somehow got blended with the true story of Fulk FitzWarin. King John and Fulk were actually childhood friends. The story goes that they got into a fight while playing chess, and John broke the chessboard over Fulk's head. Fulk then kicked John in the stomach. John eventually got back at Fulk once they were adults by giving away Fulk's land to his enemy. Fulk then murdered the enemy and became an outlaw, living in the woods and fighting off John's men for years. They later made up, until Fulk once again turned against John and sided with the barons, who made John sign the Magna Carta.

This is just one of the origin stories for the Robin Hood legend. We'll probably never know the whole truth, but Robin Hood's story has inspired storytellers for generations.

LACKLAND VS. LIONHEART

Two brothers; two memorable nicknames. Richard gets all the glory for his brave "lionhearted" adventures in the Crusades, but he wasn't actually such a superstar in real life. Despite being the king of England, he could barely speak English and only spent about six months of his life there (the Plantagenet royal family was from France and had extended their rule into England). He hated the country because it was too cold and rainy. He taxed people heavily and even declared war on his own father!

John was definitely bad, but he did do *some* things right. He was the first in his family to speak English as his first language. He built the Royal Navy, which later became England's strongest suit in becoming a conquering power. John also gave away much of England's territory in France, which actually helped England become more English. After his time, kings and barons actually spoke English and dropped their old connections to France. And signing the Magna Carta was the first step toward English democracy (even though that wasn't John's intention). In the end, some of John's minuses turned into pluses for the people of England. But he could never live down his terrible (and well-deserved) nickname.

in England back then). Annoyed, the local chiefs united against him, and John fled back to England only a few months later.

John even laughed at the priest during his own coronation. The barons of his lands in France decided to switch teams and join the king of France rather than serve him, so King John went to war with them. He lost, however, and gained the new nickname of Softsword.

The English also hated King John because he taxed them so much for his failed war. When King John picked a fight with the pope, he was banished from the Catholic Church. John retaliated by banning most church services in England for six years. This made people hate him even more, because going to church was one of the few "fun" things for ordinary people to do. Finally, the English barons forced King

John to sign the Magna Carta, which stated that even a king is not above the law. Good news for the people, bad news for kings everywhere.

BAD LUCK

King John had no intention of keeping the promises he made in the Magna Carta, so he gathered an army to fight against the barons who made him sign it. Unfortunately for him, the dauphin (prince) of France decided to invade England at just the same time. King John fled his castle, and being suspicious, he brought his entire treasury with him—jewels, gold, crowns, and all. While traveling through a marsh, the tide came in, and all those precious treasures washed away, leaving him penniless.

King John died three days later, some say from grief, some say from eating rotten peaches or from poisoning. Treasure hunters today still look for his gold in a place called "King John's Hole."

◀◀ **King John's Legacy** ▶▶

Even though he withdrew his support for it right away, the Magna Carta that King John signed was a very important document, making it possible for England to develop a government beyond the king's total control in the future.

IF YOU HAD LIVED IN KING JOHN'S ENGLAND... YOU PROBABLY WOULD HAVE:

shared your room with pigs and chickens

spent a lot of time picking lice and fleas out of your hair

had a sneaking suspicion that the old lady next door
with the hairy wart was a witch

been engaged to be married already if you were over eight years old

VLAD THE IMPALER

BAD TO THE BONE (WALLACHIA, PRESENT-DAY ROMANIA)

THREE SEPARATE REIGNS: 1448; 1456–1462; 1476
FATHER: Vlad Dracul / **MOTHER:** Cneajna
SUCCESSOR: Mihnea the Bad
OTHER NAMES: Vlad III, Dracula

• • •

WHAT WAS SO TERRIBLE ABOUT VLAD?

Vlad is best known as the (very loose) inspiration for Bram Stoker's *Dracula*. While he definitely wasn't an undead blood drinker, Vlad did display a lot of bloodthirsty behavior.

A PAWN IN THE GAME

Vlad's father was the leader of a country called Wallachia in what is now southern Romania. His father was a member of the Order of the Dragon, so Vlad's second name, Dracula, meant "son of the dragon." (Nowadays, it means "son of the demon").

Wallachia was sandwiched between Europe and the Ottoman Empire. The two superpowers went at each other constantly, and wars were fought nonstop on Vlad's home territory. When Vlad was about eleven years old, his father promised he'd support the Ottomans. To make sure he kept his word, the Ottoman sultan held Vlad and his younger brother hostage. If the father went back on his word, the captors said, the boys would be killed.

By all accounts, life as hostages wasn't bad for the boys. They received a good education. The Ottomans preferred Vlad's brother Radu (his nickname was Radu the Handsome) over him, so Vlad was said to be jealous. Once their father's loyalty was thought to be secure, the two were finally released. Radu decided to stay with the Ottomans. Vlad returned home and soon became the ruler of Wallachia.

BECOMING BAD VLAD

Once he became ruler, Vlad was as warlike as most rulers in his part of the world during that time. But he took his warring nature much, much further.

The most famous story about Vlad is that one time he invited hundreds of local warlords to a banquet. But dinner wasn't the goal of this meeting. Once these guests had eaten and were sitting back, relaxing, Vlad's guards swooped in and stabbed them all. Then they were impaled, meaning a kind of pole was stuck through their bodies in one end so it came out the other. Vlad is said to have used rounded poles instead of spiky ones so that the person would suffer for a long time before dying. One story goes that Vlad impaled hundreds on the battlefield, too, then sat down to eat among the dead and dying. Many of those impaled were displayed outside his city as a way to scare off invaders. It's said to have worked, but it must have scared off the city's residents, too!

Locals were so fearful of Vlad's vengeance that it's said they never committed crimes. There's a legend that he left a gold cup in the street overnight and no one stole it because they were afraid what would happen if they got caught.

Another terrible story about Vlad involves Ottoman ambassadors who came to visit Wallachia. It was their custom to always leave their turbans on. When Vlad demanded they remove them, they refused. He is said to have had the turbans nailed to their heads. At this point, word must have gotten around not to visit Vlad.

Vlad is also said to have bragged about all the people he killed. Estimates put that number at around 80,000 people, which would have been a large portion of the population in his country.

But when he wasn't impaling people, Vlad did normal prince things like going hunting with his friends, going to church, and signing official papers. He's said to have died by beheading on the battlefield against the Ottoman Empire, and then his head was carried back to Constantinople for display. The saying "Live by the

DRACULA'S CASTLE

Vlad's real castle in Wallachia crumbled long ago. But when tourism officials in modern-day Romania saw that there was an interest in Dracula in the late twentieth century, they looked around for a castle that they could say was his.

Bran Castle in Transylvania looks like the castle described in Bram Stoker's *Dracula*. It's located on the edge of a cliff, with turrets and sheer walls and a threatening appearance. This seemed like the perfect place to send Dracula tourists. It's possible that Vlad visited there or even was held captive there, but he certainly never lived there. Still, people call it Dracula's Castle. It is the most visited tourist attraction in Romania, and thousands of people from around the world visit each year. The castle educates people about the real history of Vlad and the region, but also plays up the spooky local legends associated with the fictional Dracula.

sword, die by the sword" applies here. After he died, people started referring to him as Vlad the Impaler, and the nickname has stuck with him throughout history.

So are the gruesome stories about Vlad true? Most of what we know about him comes from German stories from that time period, including a pamphlet, "The Frightening and Truly Extraordinary Story of a Bloodthirsty Madman Called Dracula of Wallachia." Because the Germans were his enemies, it's possible they exaggerated many of the details about Vlad's terribleness. There are stories from *his* region that paint a different picture. He is seen as a strong and brave leader for his time. Could the truth be somewhere in between?

THE ORIGINAL DRACULA?

H ow did Vlad come to be known as the original Dracula? An Irish author named Bram Stoker is responsible for this legend.

Bram Stoker never visited Transylvania (in former Wallachia). But he had read a book that was written about the area where Vlad ruled. When Stoker read about Vlad, he thought Vlad sounded like an amazing character. This set his imagination in motion. As he wrote *Dracula*, he borrowed certain aspects of Vlad's life and wove them in with local folklore from the region. In Transylvania, there was an ancient belief in people who appeared ordinary during the day, but then roamed the night as spirits to torment humans. These spirits were undead and could never rest. There were stories of blood drinkers in the region, too—people who had not been accepted into heaven were said to roam the night drinking blood from cattle (but not from humans).

Combining elements of the stories together, Stoker came up with the character of Count Dracula, a nobleman who was also a vampire, living in a crumbling castle in Transylvania. While the name Dracula links to Vlad, Stoker intentionally made Dracula different from the real ruler. *Dracula* was published in 1897, and it was an immediate hit. In the time since then, "Dracula" has also been the subject of countless movies and books.

Even though there were never any stories about Vlad being a vampire before the publication of Stoker's novel, there are some stories that associate him with the undead. For many centuries after his death, there was a local oral tradition that Vlad Dracul would come back to life one day when his country needed him.

Vlad's Legacy

While Vlad didn't really accomplish anything for his people in his time, the legends surrounding his life have helped bring tourism money to what was once his homeland.

IF YOU HAD LIVED IN VLAD'S TIME...
YOU WOULD HAVE:

believed in the Moroi, undead creatures who draw energy from the living

used a piece of linen cloth as a toothbrush, and maybe used a little crushed salt, pepper, and mint as toothpaste

left gifts for the "fate fairies" after your brother or sister was born so he or she would have a good life

BLOODY MARY TUDOR

A MALIGNED MONARCH (ENGLAND)

REIGN: 1554–1558

FATHER: Henry VIII / **MOTHER:** Catherine of Aragon

SIBLINGS: Elizabeth I and Edward VI

SUCCESSOR: Elizabeth I (see page 77)

OTHER NAMES: Mary Tudor, the Tudor Rose

WHAT WAS SO TERRIBLE ABOUT MARY?

During Queen Mary's reign, many people were burned at the stake for their religious beliefs. She put ideology above the well-being of her subjects, and that's one of the reasons she earned her bloodthirsty reputation.

FAMILY DRAMA

Every family has its issues. The Tudor family had more than most. Mary had a happy childhood—think palaces and ponies. It is said that her father, King Henry VIII, adored her. But at the same time, he really, really wanted a son. Mary was sixteen when everything changed. Because King Henry thought he might have a boy with another woman (and because divorce was illegal), he annulled his marriage to Mary's mother. He even started a new religion (the Church of England, a kind of Protestant Christianity) so he could marry again.

Mary didn't take the separation from her father well. She was not a fan of her stepmother, Anne Boleyn. She called her a witch. When Henry and Anne had a daughter—Elizabeth—Mary's "princess" title was taken away. Anne wanted her own daughter to be the only one with that official title. Anne saw Mary as a threat to Elizabeth's future and insisted that Mary serve as Elizabeth's lady-in-waiting.

But because her father still wanted a son, more family drama ensued. Mary ended up with several new stepmothers and—finally—a new half brother. When her half brother died at age fifteen, Mary became the first woman in English history to rule the country on her own. Because of that fact alone, there were a lot of people who didn't want her to succeed. Mary was destined for a bumpy ride no matter how you look at it.

BEWARE OF QUEENS BEARING GRUDGES

When she became queen, Mary seems to have seen it as an opportunity to right past wrongs. She wanted to go back in time to when her parents were still married and her father loved her best. The first thing she did was have her parents' marriage declared legal again. But instead of moving things forward for England, this brought up a lot of bad feelings from the past.

Mary was a true believer in the Catholic religion, and making England Catholic again was her top priority. To do this, she decided she'd (a) marry a Catholic king so her children would also be Catholic, and (b) get rid of the Protestants. Neither one was a popular decision.

Mary married Prince Philip of Spain (a Catholic country). People in England didn't like him. The feeling was mutual. Worse, Prince Philip didn't even like Mary! He went back to Spain soon after they were married, but not before convincing his wife to start a war with France. Bad idea. England lost horribly, and the English people blamed Mary for the defeat. Phillip also convinced Mary that she needed to take drastic measures (see below) to make sure everyone became Catholic again. Heeding his advice, Mary began her reign of terror.

H IS FOR HERETIC

Mary created a law stating that those who didn't openly embrace the Catholic faith instead of the Church of England could be burned at the stake for heresy. This punishment was chosen instead of hanging because it was supposed to remind people of the eternal fires of hell they'd face for not being believers. Around three

SISTERLY LOVE?

ome say Mary and Elizabeth really did love each other, despite their sixteen-year age difference and the complicated story of their early life. They were sisters, after all.

Elizabeth really didn't want any trouble when her sister became queen. After Mary assumed the throne, Elizabeth wrote to her to reassure her that she respected her and he wouldn't try to take her place. Publicly, she even practiced the Catholic faith so she could be seen as a loyal subject. Still, Mary's advisors told her she should get rid of Elizabeth.

Elizabeth seems to have had the last word, though. When she became queen, she supported the idea of her sister as "Bloody Mary" because it was helpful propaganda in her quest to keep England Protestant. She even made sure the ships going to the New World carried copies of a book about Mary's horrible oppression of Protestants.

Today, the two sisters are buried in adjoining chapels in Westminster Abbey, along with the inscription "Consorts in realm and tomb, we sisters Elizabeth and Mary, here lie down to sleep in hope of resurrection."

hundred heretics were burned at the stake during Mary's five-year reign. Up until this time, burning as punishment was usually the sentence for important people. Three high-level bishops (including the Archbishop of Canterbury) were burned at the stake by Mary's command. But later, even the common people weren't safe—weavers, shoemakers, fishermen—anyone could be burned for being a heretic. Mary thought that people would be so scared that they'd definitely accept her religion.

The plan backfired.

T IS FOR TRAITOR

Mary wasn't just unpopular with the people she ruled over. At court, everything was a mess. There were constant rumors about who was trying to overthrow her. Mary was a bit paranoid—and rightfully so. There actually *was* a plot to overthrow her. Sir Thomas Wyatt (son of an important diplomat) led a small force to depose her and put Elizabeth in her place. Some of Mary's advisors insisted that Elizabeth must have been involved in the plot. They arrested the young girl and imprisoned her in the Tower of London.

SURVIVOR: TUDOR ENGLAND EDITION!

Mary has been remembered mostly for all the executions and burnings carried out during her short reign. Some of the notables who met their end include her cousin, Lady Jane Grey, the "Nine-Days' Queen," and her uncle, John Dudley. Both lost their heads at the Tower of London.

Although she clearly earned her nickname Bloody Mary, Mary's father, King Henry VIII, had a much bloodier past. After all, he had two of his wives' heads chopped off! He also had some of his closest friends beheaded because they disagreed with him. Some say King Henry VIII was responsible for more than 70,000 executions during his reign. He may have gotten away with this because he was more popular than Mary or because ultimately his side (those who chose to be Protestant) prevailed and England remained a Protestant country.

And although modern-day historians call her Good Queen Bess, Queen Elizabeth actually had more people killed in her reign than Mary had killed in hers (though for different reasons and over the course of three times as many years). This includes her cousin Mary, Queen of Scots.

Mary was certainly bloody, but in a way, she was just carrying on a family tradition.

Elizabeth was held in the same place where her mother, Anne Boylen, had stayed before having her head cut off. There were other accused plotters there, too, including her cousin, Lady Jane Grey (see page 122). Jane and the others were beheaded. But Mary really didn't want to execute her sister. She begged Elizabeth to explain her innocence in writing. Elizabeth did and was eventually released and put under house arrest instead. She lived in the gatehouse of Woodstock Palace for a year and then was allowed to return to her home in Hatfield, where she continued to be kept under close supervision.

◄◄ Mary's Legacy ►►

All the drama during her reign made it hard for Mary to get things done, but she did make it possible for queens in England to hold power in exactly the same way as kings, for the first time ever.

IF YOU HAD LIVED IN MARY'S TIME...
YOU WOULD HAVE BEEN:

lucky if you lived past your first birthday. If you reached age forty, you would be considered to have lived a long life

used to a diet of bread, beer, and grainy soup

likely to go see one of the stake burnings with your family for fun

IVAN THE TERRIBLE

A RUTHLESS RULER (RUSSIA)

REIGN: 1533–1584

FATHER: Vasili III / **MOTHER:** Grand Princess Elena

SUCCESSOR: Feodor I

OTHER NAMES: Tsar Ivan IV

WHAT WAS SO TERRIBLE ABOUT IVAN?

Ivan has gone down in history as one of the worst rulers ever because of his cruelty, his strange behavior, and his lack of accomplishments. His tactics for oppressing his people were so terrible that his name has forever been associated with evil.

BECOMING TERRIBLE

To set the record straight, in Russian, Ivan's nickname was *Ivan Grozny*. In English, that *can* be translated as "Ivan the Terrible," "Ivan the Fearsome," or "Ivan the Formidable," but it can also be translated as "Ivan the Awesome" (as in inspiring awe).

TERRIBLE FATHER

Ivan's personal life was as terrible as his public life. He had six marriages, although only three were legal. It's said he wasn't a great husband or father.

But was Ivan so bad that he'd actually murder his son? The story goes that when Ivan's daughter-in-law was pregnant, Ivan told her she wasn't appropriately dressed for his court. He began hitting her with his walking stick. When Ivan's son defended his wife, Tsar Ivan killed the son (but maybe by accident).

Legend has it that when Ivan was born, there was a terrible storm in Moscow, with thunder crashing throughout the night. A priest who advised Ivan's father told him that Ivan would be wicked and that rivers of blood would flow in their country. So Ivan's life didn't get off to a great start.

Ivan had a tough childhood. He was orphaned at age eight, and those left in charge of him didn't really care about him. They set a bad example for him by murdering their enemies, among other terrible acts. It's said that Ivan often didn't have enough to eat. Could that account for his horrible childhood behavior, which is said to have included throwing cats out the upper floor windows of his palace just for fun?

Ivan was the first Russian ruler to take the title of tsar—"tsar of *all* Russia," to be exact. He thought this title sounded more important than "prince," which is what his predecessors had used for centuries. He wanted to sound more like a European or Roman emperor instead of just another monarch.

REIGN OF TERROR

Ivan wasn't completely terrible—at first—even though he had a rival executed shortly after taking the throne at age sixteen. He accomplished a few good things in his early years, such as expanding the Russian empire and developing some new administrative departments in the government.

THANKS, BUT NO THANKS

Ivan really wanted to be seen as important to the rest of the world. Legend has it that he asked Queen Elizabeth I of England (see page 77) to marry him because he thought it would boost Russia's reputation as an important country. She wrote back saying, no thanks, I'd rather stay single. On the other hand, the two countries *did* begin trading with each other around the same time, and Elizabeth and Ivan were said to have remained pen pals for years.

PLOTS! PLAGUE! POISON!

Because of his paranoia, Ivan believed those around him were plotting against him. There isn't any evidence that these plots actually existed, but he believed they did, and it led him to develop his secret police.

During Ivan's time, Russia experienced a devastating crop failure, followed by an outbreak of the plague. The plague killed thousands of people. The city of Moscow also caught fire and was invaded by the Tartars while Ivan was in power. Strangely, the tsar decided to take a break from being ruler and let the invading general be tsar for a year while he went out to the countryside for some recovery time.

Poison also played a big part in Ivan's life. His mother, Elena, and his first wife, Anastasia, were both thought to have been poisoned. When Anastasia died, some thought Ivan had done it (although it's said that she was the only person he ever really loved). Some speculate that Anastasia somehow ingested poison meant for Ivan. When Ivan's second wife, Maria, died, the suspected cause of death was—you guessed it—poison. Ivan married again after a two-year search for a wife. And his third wife's cause of death? Poison. When Ivan died, poison was also suspected to have played a part.

Modern forensic researchers have found that there was a lot of mercury in the system of both Ivan's first wife and his mother. At the time, mercury was common in both cosmetics and medicine. Mercury poisoning might account for some of Ivan's paranoia and instability. So maybe it wasn't poison after all, but rather a lack of scientific understanding that caused his mental instability and the deaths of those he loved.

But he always had a difficult personality. His main traits were paranoia and uncontrolled rage. He expressed interest only in himself. He demanded absolute loyalty from his subjects and those in his court. If he sensed betrayal of any sort, he would have the person (or people) eliminated.

IVAN'S SECRET POLICE

van didn't get his reputation for terribleness on his own. Much of it came from the ruthless secret police force he developed in order to spy on his subjects. This secret police force was called the *oprichnina* (oh-prich-NEE-na), and they were authorized to do whatever they wanted—all in the name of protecting Ivan.

The oprichnina was formed after one of Ivan's best friends (a nobleman) betrayed him. At this point, Ivan became very paranoid and decided he needed a secret police squad to prevent anyone from betraying him ever again. He was out to get *all* nobles after that one incident. Ivan recruited young men from the lower classes, who had to prove they had no connections to nobility, to serve on the force. Once they were chosen, the new members had to take an oath to protect the tsar.

The members of the oprichnina were terrifying to see. They wore dark robes. Around the necks of their horses hung two items: a severed dog's head and a broom. This was meant to symbolize that they'd tear people to shreds like dogs and sweep them away if they misbehaved or plotted against the tsar.

If a member of the secret police didn't like someone, they could accuse him of plotting against Ivan, take his land, and kill him. They terrorized everyone, but especially the nobles.

Eventually, Ivan lost control of his secret police, and he had its leaders killed. But it was said that every noble family in Russia had lost at least one family member to their brutality.

Ivan was petty and vindictive. The beautiful St. Basil's Cathedral in Moscow was built during his reign. But he is said to have blinded the architect afterward so that he couldn't build something as beautiful for anyone else.

Ivan started several (mostly unsuccessful) wars during his reign. One of them lasted twenty-five years and left the country bankrupt. But it was the widespread oppression against his people (see below) that cemented Ivan's "terrible" reputation. In one town alone (Novogard), he's said to have had tens of thousands of his citizens killed, including women and children. Today, he's known as one of the most evil rulers ever.

A DEADLY GAME OF CHESS

Ivan died in 1584 while playing chess. Some say that he was poisoned (or that maybe the chess set was poisoned). Or perhaps all that mercury he had been ingesting, over time, may have done him in. It's also possible that he could have suffered a stroke, a common cause of death for someone his age.

◀◀ Ivan's Legacy ▶▶

Ivan's secret police are said to have inspired the KGB, the Soviet secret police that terrorized people in the USSR (the Union of Soviet Socialist Republics, including Russia and its allied countries) in the twentieth century.

IF YOU HAD LIVED IN IVAN'S TIME...
YOU MAY HAVE:

eaten a lot of cabbage soup

used hand warmers to get you through the winter (these were little metal cases with hot coals inside them to stuff in your gloves)

ice-skated by tying pieces of animal bones to your shoes

CATHERINE DE' MEDICI

THE SERPENT QUEEN:
MURDEROUS OR MISUNDERSTOOD? (FRANCE)

REIGN: 1547–1589

FATHER: Lorenzo II, Duke of Urbino / **MOTHER:** Madeline de la Tour D'Auverge

SUCCESSOR: Henri III

OTHER NAMES: The Duchessina, the Black Queen, the Maggot from Italy's Tomb, the Merchant's Daughter

• • •

WHAT WAS SO TERRIBLE ABOUT CATHERINE?

Catherine's time at the Louvre palace was full of drama and intrigue, including the St. Bartholomew's Day Massacre, which led to thousands of murders across France for months. But her ruthless reputation might not have been entirely justified.

BAD BEGINNING

Born to one of Italy's most prominent families (the Medicis), Catherine's childhood was disruptive, to put it mildly. Both her parents died of illnesses by the time she was just three weeks old! She then went to live with her grandmother. When her grandmother died, she moved in with her aunt. Because of political unrest, she had to move again—this time to Florence, the city her family ruled (see page 52). The Medicis were on the outs, and anger against them was directed at Catherine. People leveled death threats against her and screamed at her in the streets. She never forgot this frightening experience, and some say her questionable behavior in later years sprang from this incident in her youth.

FASHION QUEEN

Catherine is credited with introducing three important fashion trends to France: underwear, high heels, and perfumed gloves. In Italy, women rode horses sidesaddle and ladies were often assisted in dismounting by gentlemen or servants. They wore underwear to avoid any unintentional exposure while getting on and off their horses. In France, there was no such thing as underwear until noblewomen heard about it from Catherine, and it became a trend.

Catherine is thought to have been less than five feet tall, and her short stature bothered her. She wanted to appear taller at her wedding, so she had a platform shoe designed for that purpose. Women had been wearing platform shoes in Italy for a while, but they were impossible to walk in. Only noblewomen wore them, and they had to hold on to their servants as they walked. Catherine's walkable high-heeled shoes (similar to the modern design) became a fashion trend and all the noble ladies started wearing them. After Catherine's death, however, it was only men who wore high-heeled shoes for the next several hundred years.

Catherine also brought the scented gloves trend to France. It was a time when there were a lot of bad odors in daily life, and the gloves helped people stay fresh smelling. Unfortunately, even this innocent fashion choice was used against Catherine. When her daughter's future mother-in-law was found dead, people said Catherine had sent her a pair of poisoned gloves as a gift in order to kill her.

CHILD BRIDE

For political reasons, Catherine was married off to Prince Henri of France. They were both only fourteen years old. It was a grand wedding with gold and velvet and jewels and even a real lion as a present!

Unfortunately, Henri was already in love with a woman who was nineteen years older than him. Catherine soon caught on that she wasn't going to win

Henri's love and came to an agreement with his consort, Diane. The three of them lived, if not happily ever after, then at least peaceably together until Henri died in a jousting accident.

By that time, Catherine and Henri had ten children together. Three of Catherine's sons became King of France at young ages: Francis II (made king at fifteen and dead a year later), Charles IX (king for fourteen years till his death at age twenty-four), and Henri III (said to be her favorite—king from age twenty-three until his death at age thirty-seven). Because the boys were so young when they assumed the throne, Catherine served as regent and unofficial advisor for them.

It's said that Catherine learned what she knew about ruling from her countryman Nicolo Machiavelli, the Italian philosopher whose most famous quotes include "It is better to be feared than loved. You cannot be both," and "Politics have no relations to morals."

THAT GIRL IS POISON

Catherine's nickname, The Serpent Queen, came about not just from what was seen as her sneaky moves, but from the idea that she was venomous and liked to poison people.

Although there's no evidence she ever poisoned anyone, there were reasons for this reputation. She was a Medici and their use of poison (see page 62) was well known, even in France. It wasn't just her family, though. The French thought of poison as the Italian weapon of choice. There were also rumors that Catherine had a secret poison stash in her room. If you visit the palace at Blois today, you can see the two hundred concealed cabinets where she is said to have kept her poisons.

A STRANGE STRANGER

The French people never really took to Catherine as a ruler. They considered Italy their enemy and looked down on her because the Medici didn't seem like real royalty to them. Her nickname, The Merchant's Daughter, was a dig at the Medicis' status.

Catherine was really into astrology, a hobby that high-ranking French officials found off-putting. She even consulted the famed Nostradamus about her future, and he had some pretty accurate predictions for her. People said she practiced black magic and had an all-woman team of spies who reported to her. Some rumors about her were even worse: she was said to eat children!

A BLOODY WEDDING DAY

During Catherine's time, there was a lot of religious tension in France between Catholics and Protestants. To try to make peace, Catherine arranged for her Catholic daughter Marguerite to marry the Protestant king Henry of Navarre. During the wedding celebrations in Paris, there was an attempt on the life of a Protestant leader. What happened next is up for debate, but helped seal Catherine's reputation as a terrible ruler.

THE SELFIE QUEEN

Catherine loved to have self-portraits painted. (Nowadays, she probably would have loved taking selfies!) Like any proud mother, she also loved looking at pictures of her kids and had their portraits painted regularly throughout their lives.

Being a Medici, she was a big supporter of the arts and had lots of sculptures commissioned, too. One of the most famous was a statue of three women supporting an urn raised above their heads. The urn contained the *actual* heart of Henri, Catherine's husband. The statue is now on display at the Louvre in Paris, but the heart has since been removed.

Some say that Catherine (and her son Charles, who was king) secretly met with advisors and decided to wipe out all the Protestant leaders while they were in town for the wedding. Others say that the plan wasn't that extensive and that things got out of hand quickly. Either way, many wedding guests were murdered. It has been called the St. Bartholomew's Day Massacre. Naturally, the Protestants were upset. They believed the whole wedding had been arranged just to get them to come to Paris to kill them. That's no way to treat your guests.

Things got much worse after this terrible "celebration" ended. Killings between the Catholics and the Protestants spread throughout the country for months, even after there was a royal decree to end them. It was widely believed that Catherine was responsible for the whole thing, so the people's hatred for Catherine was cemented.

◄◄ Catherine's Legacy ►►

In addition to possibly being responsible for the killings in the St. Bartholomew's Day Massacre, Catherine did some other pretty terrible things during her time as a regent, including having her daughter locked up and ordering her son-in-law to be murdered. But her reputation certainly suffered from being a powerful woman and a foreigner in a place and time when that was a serious disadvantage. In the end, she probably wasn't as serpentlike as she's portrayed to be.

IF YOU HAD LIVED IN CATHERINE'S TIME... YOU MAY HAVE:

survived the new outbreak of the bubonic plague that killed nearly 100,000 Europeans

been a resident of the world's largest city (Paris)

witnessed the construction of the Tuileries palace and gardens in the City of Lights

MAD IBRAHIM I

A STRANGE SULTAN
(OTTOMAN EMPIRE, PRESENT-DAY TURKEY)

REIGN: 1640–1648

FATHER: Sultan Ahmet / **MOTHER:** Maypeyker Kösem

SUCCESSOR: Mehmed IV

OTHER NAMES: The Red Mullet (because of his habit of feeding gold coins to fish)

•••

WHAT WAS SO TERRIBLE ABOUT IBRAHIM?

Ibrahim wasn't up to the task of ruling one of the world's biggest empires. He may not have been outright cruel, but he did make some terrible decisions, from starting ineffective and costly wars to listening to bad advice and being open to corruption.

THE BOY IN THE GOLDEN CAGE

Ibrahim's life got off to a tough start because of a tradition that started long before his birth.

The Ottomans had a pretty bad way of picking the next sultan after the previous one died. Whoever could physically get to the throne first won the right to rule. Then the winner ordered all his brothers to be strangled with a silk cord so they couldn't try to overthrow him. This was a serious problem because in a sultan's family there might be dozens of siblings—sometimes as many as a hundred! If you happened to be one of the unlucky brothers, life was stressful, always waiting for the

A RACE TO THE DEATH

— • — • — • — • — • —

S trangling by silk cord was not a great way to go, but there was a worse fate for members of the Ottoman Court accused of serious wrongdoing. The accused would be summoned to the central gate to meet with the head gardener. After a brief chat, the person under suspicion was handed a cup of the delicious, fruity sherbet. If the sherbet was white, he was in the clear. If it was red, however, he was sentenced to death.

There was one last way to escape death, but the accused had to think (and move) fast. If he could run down through the gardens and reach the fish-market gate of the palace before the head gardener did, his life would be spared. He would be banished instead of being thrown into the river. Believe it or not, some fleet-footed men won the race. One in particular was so widely admired for winning that he was later appointed governor in one of the empire's provinces.

moment when someone would come up from behind and strangle you. It was no way to live.

This strangle-your-brother tradition went on for years until one sultan decided he just couldn't do it. One of his brothers was developmentally disabled, and he could not bring himself to hurt him. Instead, he had a room built for him called a *kafe,* or golden cage. It was part of the harem (or women's section of the palace). It was kind of like an apartment, but the windows were only on the second floor. Food was delivered through a small slot. The *kafe* was surrounded by armed guards, so it was also kind of like a prison cell. The first resident of the *kafe* lived there with his grandmother for the rest of his life. While there, he learned to do macramé to pass the time. That became one of the most popular activities for sultans who were locked up in the *kafe* throughout the years.

Future generations took on the tradition of locking up brothers instead of killing them, too. One sultan's brother lived in the *kafe* for fifty years. But sometimes the boys or men made it out and to freedom. Ibrahim was one who did.

As Ibrahim's brother, the sultan, was dying, he asked their mother who would take over for him. He wanted anyone but Ibrahim. She lied to him and told him it would be his nephew. Then she called for Ibrahim to be released so he could ascend the throne.

After all that time in the golden cage, Ibrahim wasn't really prepared to do anything as important as ruling a huge empire. It's said that when he was summoned to be released, he thought he was being tricked and wouldn't even open the door, in case someone was on the other side holding a silk cord. Ibrahim's mother said that he "had to be coaxed out like a kitten." When he finally came out, Ibrahim is said to have run through the halls screaming with joy about the death of his brother.

THE SURPRISING STORY OF SUGAR CUBE

Ibrahim once told his aides to find him "the biggest woman in the world" to add to his harem (the group of women at his palace). They did their best, bringing a three-hundred-pound girl to him. She was perfect for Ibrahim, and he nicknamed her Sugar Cube. The two became very close—too close, his advisors thought. They believed she held too much power over him.

Because there wasn't a whole lot else to do, the women in Ibrahim's harem gossiped a lot. Sugar Cube heard a rumor that the consort of one of the other women was conspiring against Ibrahim. Ibrahim is said to have overreacted when she told him of the conspiracy. He ordered all the women in the harem to be sewn into sacks and thrown into the river. The story goes that when Ibrahim's mother, Kösem, found out about it, she was really angry and had Sugar Cube strangled. But another story says that Sugar Cube lived until much later until someone added chopped-up hair and glass to her coffee and she choked.

STRANGE WAYS

Ibrahim was probably not mad, as his nickname implies. But he *was* peculiar. And he had very little interest in ruling over an empire. That worked out all right because his mother was really doing all of the heavy lifting as ruler for him.

Ibrahim's main preoccupation was collecting furs. His empire covered a vast territory, so he asked his representatives around the realm to find the best furs available and to send them to him. Stranger than that, he also had capes made from the fur of his own palace cats.

Ibrahim's other obsession was grooming. He loved to work on his beard. He oiled it with ambergris (a rare and costly scent made from whale vomit) and wove jewels into it.

Reports also said Ibrahim spent a lot of time throwing gold coins into the Bosporus (the river that runs by the palace) in order to feed the fish. He would often stand on the balcony and shoot arrows at unsuspecting passersby outside the palace walls for sport as well.

When he did get involved in government, it didn't go well. He spent money recklessly. To pay for his fur habit, he instituted a new tax that his subjects called the Fur Tax. Most people didn't want to contribute their hard-earned money to keep Ibrahim in furs.

Ibrahim started a few unsuccessful wars. Famine and plague spread across the empire. But it may have been his obsession with one of the women in his harem that did him in.

After the horrifying incident with the harem (see page 139), a leader called the Grand Mufti overthrew Ibrahim, and he was sent back to the golden cage. Ten days later, the inevitable finally happened—he was strangled with a silk cord.

Ibrahim's Legacy

Ibrahim didn't provide the leadership needed for his vast empire. Both the finances and the governance suffered during his reign and it was said to be the beginning of the end for the Ottoman Empire.

IF YOU HAD LIVED IN IBRAHIM'S TIME... YOU MIGHT HAVE:

enjoyed eating horse meat

seen snake charmers in your local market

avoided drinking coffee in public—it was punishable by death

SULTAN ISMAIL THE BLOODTHIRSTY

A FEARSOME FATHER (MOROCCO)

REIGN: 1672–1727

FATHER: Sharif ibn Ali / **MOTHER:** Unknown

SUCCESSOR: Abu'l Abbas Ahmad

OTHER NAMES: Moulay Ismail Ibn Sharif, the Warrior King, the Sun King

WHAT WAS SO TERRIBLE ABOUT ISMAIL?

Ismail didn't think much of his subjects. He's said to have compared them to rats in a basket. "If I don't keep shaking the basket, they'll gnaw their way through," he is reported to have said. He continually showed his disdain for his people through murderous acts throughout his reign.

THE ACCIDENTAL SULTAN

Ismail wasn't expecting to become sultan. He was the seventh son of the reigning king of the Alaouite dynasty. But one day, while riding a horse through a garden during a party, the brother hit his head on a low-hanging branch, fell from his horse, and died. His death provided Ismail with an opportunity. He beat out eighty-three brothers and half-brothers to take the throne by immediately seizing the treasury and declaring himself sultan.

When he first took the throne, Ismail is said to have displayed four hundred heads on pikes outside the city of Fez to give folks there an idea what his reign would be like.

DON'T EVEN LOOK AT ME

One of the first rules that Ismail enacted as sultan was that no one was permitted to look him directly in the eye. Not only that, but if anyone looked at one of his wives or concubines, that person would be put to death. To avoid such a gruesome fate, men visiting Ismail's court would lie face down on the ground without looking up if they thought any women would be present.

In addition to four wives and five hundred concubines, Ismail had an almost countless number of children (see below). One son in particular was supposed to inherit the throne once Ismail died. One of Ismail's wives didn't like the boy. She told Ismail that his son planned to depose him (that wasn't true). Ismail then had the boy's left arm and right leg cut off as a warning. Sadly, it was more than a warning: the boy died of blood loss.

BLOODTHIRSTY REIGN

Ismail usually wore the colors white and green. But if he was in a bad mood, he wore yellow. When he was seen wearing yellow, people would become terrified and run away. Ismail was said to have had a terrible temper. No one knew what would set him off. One story goes that he had a beautiful new gate built in the city of Fez, and he asked the architect if it could have been more beautiful. When the architect said yes, Ismail had him executed on the spot.

A VERY BUSY FATHER'S DAY

• - • - • - • - •

It's said that Ismail had 1,000 children. That's thought to be more children than any other man in human history. While this claim sounds like it might just be an exaggeration, the *Guinness Book of World Records* has verified at least 888 of them. Modern studies indicate that it is indeed possible that he may have had as many as 1,042 children, possibly even a few more.

PUT A RING ON IT

One of Ismail's ambassadors made a lengthy trip to France to negotiate a treaty. Morocco and France were allies because they both hated Spain. France agreed to help push the remaining Spanish presence out of Morocco if Morocco would stop taking French sailors prisoner. During his visit, the Moroccan ambassador encountered Princess Marie Anne de Bourbon. He developed a friendship with her and told Ismail of her beauty once he returned to Morocco. Because negotiations with France weren't going well, Ismail suggested maybe he should marry the princess—that was always a good way to unite kingdoms. The King of France did not grant this request, however, but the two countries did enjoy a brief alliance.

After getting on his horse, Ismail would often turn to the servant who helped him get his foot in the stirrup and lop his head off with his sword. He had many cats that he was said to pamper most of the time, but might also publicly execute them if he was in a bad mood.

Ismail held grudges, too. When one of his rivals in Marrakech escaped, he maintained a manhunt for him that lasted ten years until the rival was finally found and executed.

Ismail was sultan for fifty-five long years, making him one of the longest-reigning leaders in history. It's estimated that during this long reign, 30,000 people were killed on his command.

◄◄ Ismail's Legacy ►►

While he didn't get his bloodthirsty reputation for nothing, Ismail is also remembered for helping Morocco gain its independence from the Ottoman Empire and for uniting different parts of his country.

PIRATICAL PRISONERS

During Ismail's reign, piracy was at its height up and down the Barbary Coast (the part of North Africa bordering the Mediterranean, including some of Morocco). It was common for pirates to take the crew from captured ships prisoner and sell them as slaves or hold them for ransom. There's a report that a ship with four hundred sailors was captured in Iceland and sold to Ismail's court. Because of this, there were many European slaves held captive in Morocco. Ismail had enough slaves that he even developed a slave army he would send out to war so that his own subjects didn't have to be killed.

Much of what we know about life as a slave under Ismail's reign comes from a book called *The History of the Long Captivity and Adventures of Thomas Pellow*. The book was dictated to the writer by an English man who was taken captive at age eleven. He spent twenty-three years as a slave at Ismail's court before he escaped.

Thomas describes dungeons under Ismail's compound where prisoners were shackled to the walls at night so they had to sleep standing up. After some time, Thomas was promoted to a special private army belonging to Ismail, called the Black Guard. As a guard member, he was given a wife as a present and later they had a child together. (According to Thomas, Sultan Ismail thought slaves would be less likely to run away if they had a family.) Eventually, Thomas was able to board a ship and escape back to England, where his story became a bestseller for many years.

THE VERSAILLES OF THE SOUTH

Ismail was a big fan of King Louis XIV of France, and the two enjoyed a long correspondence. Sultan Ismail so admired the French King that he wanted to make Meknes (his ruling city) an homage to the great palace at Versailles.

Building up the city became a major project during Ismail's reign. He did it with the tens of thousands of slaves that he had acquired either through taking them hostage after battles or purchasing them from pirates (see page 146). Sometimes he would have a palace built, then torn down and rebuilt just because he could.

By the time Ismail died, Meknes was definitely on par with Versailles. There were fifty palaces inside the city walls, which stretched for over twenty miles and had twenty entrance gates. After he died, Ismail's grandson moved Morocco's capital to Marrakech and Meknes faded into history. Today, many of the monuments built during Ismail's time are preserved, including the beautiful Bab Mansour gate, considered one of the best examples of Moorish architecture (and a UNESCO World Heritage site).

IF YOU HAD LIVED IN ISMAIL'S TIME . . . YOU:

might have considered piracy a viable career option

might have worn a talisman with a red string
to protect yourself from the evil eye

wouldn't whistle inside your house—it was considered bad luck

QUEEN RANAVALONA THE CRUEL

NOTABLY NOTORIOUS (MADAGASCAR)

REIGN: 1782–1861

HUSBAND: Radama / **MOTHER:** Unknown

SUCCESSOR: Radama II

OTHER NAMES: Ranavalona the Bloody, the Devil Incarnate

· · ·

WHAT WAS SO TERRIBLE ABOUT RANAVALONA?

"She is certainly one of the proudest and cruel women on the face of the earth, and her whole history is a record of bloodshed and deeds of horror," said Ida Pfeiffer, an Austrian explorer who met Ranavalona during her reign. The queen's bloodthirsty reputation was built on decades of doing away with anyone who disagreed with her.

PLOT TWIST

Ranavalona's life started out fairly ordinary. Ramavo (her name when she was a little girl) was the daughter of commoners. When her father heard of a plot to overthrow the then current Madagascan king, he informed the monarch. To reward Ramavo's father, the king said that Ramavo could marry his son, the prince Radama. In this way, Ramavo became the first of Radama's twelve wives.

BECOMING RANAVALONA

Radama became king upon his father's death, and Ramavo rose in power along with him. However, King Radama and Ramavo never really got along, and they

THE BUFFALO HUNT

One of the most famous stories about Ranavalona centers on an 1845 buffalo hunt. According to her wishes, around 50,000 members of her court—including servants and slaves—took off looking for buffalo. They brought barely any food or supplies with them on the hunt. They also had to build a road to get where they were going. Along the way, around 10,000 of the hunting party died from starvation and disease. Since they had to keep moving, there was no time to bury the dead. The road became full of dead bodies, one eyewitness said, and after the four-month expedition, no buffalo were ever found and killed.

never had children. Ramavo especially didn't like the way her husband let so many foreigners come into Madagascar as missionaries or businesspeople. When Radama died after eighteen years on the throne, his nephew Rakotobe was supposed to take over according to the country's rules of succession. But Radama swooped in and declared herself queen and ruler of Madagascar, to be known as Ranavalona. Then she had Rakotobe, his mother, and many of his other relatives killed, getting her reign off to a murderous start.

AND STAY OUT!

Ranavalona closed the door to Madagascar for the British and French, breaking trade agreements and kicking missionaries out of the country. She wrote a letter to the two countries that went something like this:

"Dear British and French People: Thanks for stopping by our island! We appreciate some of the stuff you shared with us. I especially like the French fashion! We are going to take a pass on the new languages. The religion stuff is a hard no for me. We've already got one. While you're here, feel free to do what you do, but don't try to convert us. You're wasting your time. We'll never change our beliefs and if any of my subjects try to follow your customs instead of ours, they will be killed."

To make sure the message was taken seriously, she had the heads of French and English soldiers (who had been killed in battles) mounted on pikes and displayed on the beach so that their countrymen's passing ships would see them and be frightened away. In time, she banished *all* French and British people from the country—all except one. Ranavalona fell in love with a French sailor who was shipwrecked and washed up on the shore. He became one of the country's most powerful people over time and built a French-style palace for the queen (she had a bit of a love-hate relationship with everything French).

THE WAR AT HOME

Ranavalona was tough on foreigners, but she was even tougher on her own people.

Some had converted to Christianity during the reigns of the previous kings. Now, Ranavalona demanded they return to the traditional belief system, based on ancestor worship and local deities. If they didn't, they were taken to a place called The Rock of Hurling, a giant cliff. Eyewitnesses described the gruesome things that

TRIAL BY ORDEAL

Many cultures in the past used "trial by ordeal" to determine a person's guilt or innocence. When accused of a crime, a person would have to undergo a test of some sort. If they lived, they were innocent. If they died, obviously they had been guilty.

During Ranavalona's time, those accused of a crime were required to drink a poison extracted from the tagena plant. The accused person was fed three chicken skins along with the poison. If all three chicken skins were vomited up, the person was innocent. If they kept anything down, they were guilty of sorcery. Between 20 percent and 50 percent of those who did the test ended up dying. During Ranavalona's reign, it's thought that 100,000 people died this way—which was about 20 percent of the population.

THE QUEEN'S BATH

One of the stranger stories about Ranavalona involves her love of soap. While she hated just about everything foreigners brought to her island, soap was the exception. Two British missionaries reported that when they told her the many things they would teach her subjects—Greek, Hebrew, the Bible—the queen politely declined, stating that her people didn't need to learn any dead languages. There was one thing she did want them to teach her people, however, and that was the art of soap making. They were able to do so with some effort.

The queen used the soap during the *fadroana*—the annual bathing ritual. On this morning of the first day of the year, she would be anointed with rooster blood, then take a purifying bath. Ranavalona conducted this ritual on her balcony, bathing behind a screen. When she was done, she sprinkled the bath water over the side of the wall into the crowd. (Having some of the bath water land on you was considered good luck for the coming year.)

happened there: the condemned were attached to ropes and then launched over the edge; some sang church hymns as they fell. There was even a report of a rainbow appearing over the spot where they'd fallen. Some were boiled or buried alive. As many as 30,000 citizens were executed each year during Ranavalona's reign. Some of those whose lives were spared were sold into slavery.

Ranavalona also started a series of civil wars that wiped out a good portion of the population. She didn't do much in terms of helping her people, so a lot of them died of disease during her time as well. The island's population decreased by between 50 percent and 75 percent during her reign because of the wars, disease, and the brutal executions she carried out.

Interesting fact: Ranavalona's son was secretly a Christian, and he actually wrote to Napoleon III of France, inviting him to invade the island to get rid of her—that's how bad she really was.

Queen Ranavalona lived to a ripe old age. But even in death, she caused catastrophe. At her funeral, a barrel of gunpowder exploded, several buildings caught fire, and several of those there to witness her burial ended up dying.

Ranavalona's Legacy

While she's remembered outside her country as ruthless, opinions in Madagascar are mixed about Ranavalona's reign. There are many who agree that choosing to keep her country independent was a good goal. However, the queen went about it in a terrible way. Today, in Madagascar, a woman who is considered to be loud-mouthed or demanding or a strict mother is called a Ranavalona as an insult.

IF YOU HAD LIVED IN RANAVALONA'S TIME... YOU WOULD HAVE:

lived through the infamous "year without a summer," when a volcanic explosion in Indonesia in 1815 caused weather changes in 1816 that ruined crops and caused food shortages

witnessed slave ships coming and going from the island

believed that lemurs were magical protector animals

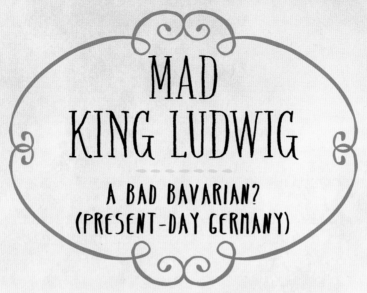

MAD KING LUDWIG

A BAD BAVARIAN?
(PRESENT-DAY GERMANY)

REIGN: 1864–1886

FATHER: Maximilian II / **MOTHER:** Marie

SUCCESSOR: Otto

OTHER NAMES: The Fairytale King, the Swan King, the Dream King

WHAT WAS SO TERRIBLE ABOUT LUDWIG?

He spent all of his kingdom's money and then started borrowing from others to satisfy his obsession for building castles. He definitely had some peculiar behaviors. But he may have been more of a victim than a villain.

A LONELY BOY

By all accounts, Ludwig had an unhappy childhood. He spent more time with governesses and tutors than his parents. He liked playing make-believe games and lived in a world of his imagination. He became King of Bavaria when he was just eighteen.

LIVING IN A DREAM

Ludwig wasn't exactly born in the wrong place, but he may have been born in the wrong time. It's said that he found his own time boring and often wished he could have been king in an earlier time—like maybe around the time of King Arthur. He loved the story of the Holy Grail and he loved medieval times in Germany. He also loved France during the reign of Louis XIV. He liked the idea of being the "Moon King," a kind of alter ego to Louis XIV's "Sun King." That might explain why he usually slept during the day and traveled under cover of darkness. Sometimes Ludwig would even wear historical costumes as his carriage rolled through the night, pretending to be a king of a bygone era!

Ludwig was a supporter of the arts and invited musicians and opera singers to perform at his castles. Strangely, at these performances, he was typically the only audience member. He especially loved the operas by Richard Wagner. He became Wagner's biggest fan. Wagner even wrote the opera "Parsifal" for Ludwig. It's based on the story of King Arthur, one of Ludwig's favorites. Ludwig was such a supporter of Wagner's that he lent him a lot of money and ended up going into debt himself to get Wagner out of financial trouble.

Ludwig didn't like the actual *job* of being king, though. His advisors complained that he didn't really read the paperwork they gave him. Because he'd been distracted with his personal interests, Ludwig didn't take a strong stand on issues. For example, during his reign, many German kingdoms became unified into one empire, with Ludwig's uncle as emperor. Although many of his advisors disagreed, Ludwig signed a letter joining the new German empire. This wasn't a very popular decision, although, realistically, he didn't have much of a choice.

OUT OF MONEY, OUT OF TIME

Ludwig used up his personal money by building castles. Then he used the government's money to keep building more castles. After that ran out, he borrowed money from other European royal families, something his government found particularly embarrassing. When he couldn't pay his debts back, foreign banks threatened to seize the castles built with borrowed money.

Ludwig racked up debt that would be in the tens of millions of dollars today, but he was still working on plans for new castles. His cabinet of advisors finally thought enough was enough and told him so. He said he'd fire them all, and that if they didn't let him complete his projects, he'd kill himself. That's when his advisors decided to take action.

The king's advisors hired a psychiatrist, not to really find out whether Ludwig *was* insane, but to *confirm* their belief that he was. After all, madness was said to run in the family (Ludwig's brother Otto had been kept from the public eye most of his life because he was believed to be mad).

The psychiatrist didn't even meet with the king before giving his diagnosis. He took secret notes from servants and met with aides at night behind Ludwig's back. What he heard wasn't terribly bad. Ludwig insisted on eating outside regardless of the weather. He refused milk in his coffee. He had threatened to have a servant deported to America. The psychiatrist determined that Ludwig suffered from paranoia. He declared that Ludwig was incapable of ruling. "He is teetering like a blind man without guidance on the verge of a precipice," the psychiatrist wrote.

Declaring the king insane wasn't really something that was allowed under the country's constitution, but the cabinet did it anyway. They took action very quickly, perhaps to make sure Ludwig couldn't object, and on June 10, 1886, Ludwig was abducted by members of his government and locked away in Berg Palace as a madman.

BAVARIAN MURDER MYSTERY

Ludwig was found dead by the side of Lake Starnberg on June 13, 1886, along with the body of the psychiatrist who had diagnosed him. Court officials said that the idea of having his kingdom taken away drove him to suicide. But did Ludwig really kill himself? People have been trying to answer that question for more than one hundred years.

Some said that Ludwig murdered his doctor and then drowned himself. Some say Ludwig didn't drown—he was thought to be a strong swimmer, and reports said there was no water found in his lungs. Fishermen on the lake reported hearing shots at the time of Ludwig's death. Some say that Ludwig was murdered and that the

THE SWAN KING'S CASTLES

Ludwig's castles were his life's work. They were inspired by legends, fairy tales, and the major palaces and castles of other rulers who Ludwig admired. Although there were more, these three are the most famous.

Schloss Neuschwanstein

This might be the most famous castle in the world. Nestled in the Bavarian Alps, it really does look like something from a fairy tale, with tall, thin towers of different heights. It took over two decades to build and actually wasn't even finished in Ludwig's lifetime. Inside, the castle is decorated with frescos that illustrate medieval stories as well as the story of the Swan Knight from *Parsifal*, the opera Wagner wrote for Ludwig. To try to earn back the money spent on the castle, the government opened it to visitors just a few weeks after Ludwig's death, even though it wasn't finished. Neuschwanstein is said to be the inspiration for the Cinderella castles at the Disney theme parks.

Schloss Herrenchiemsee

Because he admired Louis XIV so much, Ludwig modeled this castle after the Palace of Versailles (located outside of Paris). Like Versailles, its lavishly decorated interior features crystal chandeliers, brocade fabrics, frescoed ceilings, and a hall of mirrors. The gardens are designed like French gardens, with fountains and walking paths.

Schloss Linderhof

This castle is inspired by the palaces of eighteenth-century France. There's a lake in the front with a fountain and golden statue at its center. It's the smallest of Ludwig's castles and the only one finished before he died.

psychiatrist was shot because he was a witness to the heinous crime. It's possible that we'll never really know how Ludwig met his fate.

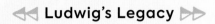

◄◄ Ludwig's Legacy ►►

While they were places of retreat and solitude during his time, Ludwig's castles are now among the most visited tourist attractions in Europe, with millions of visitors each year. Even though they resulted in great debts in his lifetime, now the castles are big money makers.

Although he died more than a century ago, new theories on his death continue to surface. We'll probably never know the truth about Ludwig's life and death. Ludwig is reported to have said to his nanny: "I want to remain an eternal mystery to myself and others." That has certainly come to pass.

IF YOU HAD LIVED IN LUDWIG'S TIME... YOU MIGHT HAVE:

been among the first to have electric lights (if you were wealthy, that is)

completed your education after eight years in school

known someone who had immigrated to the United States (if you hadn't done so yourself)

THE ROGUES GALLERY of
OTHER NOTABLY NOTORIOUS

Antiochus IV Epiphanes, the Wicked

(Ancient Greece: 175–164 BCE)

He murdered a rival and persecuted the Jews, a story which was the basis for the tale of the first Hanukkah.

Christian the Cruel (Denmark and Norway: 1513–1523)

Also known as Christian the Tyrant, he was responsible for the Stockholm Bloodbath, a mass murder of Swedish nobility.

Conomor the Cursed (Roman Brittany: 540–555)

He had several people murdered, including his brother, three wives, and a woman who refused to marry him.

Constantine V, the Dung-Named

(The Byzantine Empire: 741–775)

He had his enemies killed in gruesome ways. Constantine V got his nickname from a story about having a dirty diaper in a church while he was being baptized as a baby.

Foelke the Cruel (Frisia, present-day Germany: 1389–1419)

The cruel acts attributed to her (such as executing hundreds of prisoners without cause) may have actually been committed by her son, for whom she acted as regent.

Fredegunde the Bloodthirsty (France: 584–597)

She had her enemies murdered with poisoned axes and slammed her daughter's neck in a chest of jewels to kill her.

Isabella, the She Wolf (France: 1308–1327)

She led an invasion of England and killed her husband so she could rule with her lover.

Nang Keo Phimpa the Cruel (Laos: 1428–1437)

She had several of her nephews killed before ascending to the throne herself.

Pedro the Cruel (Spain: 1350–1369)

He is best known for holding grudges and murdering people, including his brother. He is also known as Pedro the Just.

Suriyenthrathibodi, the Tiger King (Thailand: 1703–1709)

As evil as a tiger, he is said to have used humans as bait for sharks and sawfish—among other awful deeds.

Vuk, the Fiery Dragon Wolf (Serbia: 1471–1485)

People said this Serbian king could actually breathe fire, but he may have gotten this somewhat mythical reputation after he betrayed a local prince.

Yazdgerd the Wicked (Persia: 421–399 BCE)

He brought peace to his region, but he did so by shaking hands with the enemy (Rome), and his own people never forgave him.

GLOSSARY

ABDICATE: to give up the throne

ALLY: someone who works in partnership and cooperation with another

ANNUL: to cancel or make invalid

BANKRUPT: unable to repay debts

COLONNADE: a covered row of columns, often part of a pathway connecting more than one building or parts of a building or surrounding a courtyard

CONCUBINE: a woman who is not a wife, but who lives with a man and with a lower status than a wife

CONFUCIAN PRINCIPLES: values that reflect the teachings of Confucius

CONFUCIUS: Chinese philosopher whose ideas had a strong influence on Chinese culture

CONQUER: to defeat in a military battle

CONSORT: a companion of a monarch or ruler

CONSTITUTIONAL MONARCHY: a system of government in which there is a monarch whose power is limited by a constitution

COURTIER: a person in attendance at a royal court, usually as an advisor

CRUSADES: a series of medieval military campaigns that took Christians from Europe to the Middle East to try to take the area around Jerusalem from Muslim rule

CUNEIFORM: an ancient form of writing used in Mesopotamia and Persia

DECIPHER: to translate or decode ancient writings into a language that's understood

DEPOSE: to remove forcibly from a position of power

EDICT: an official declaration

FRATRICIDE: killing a brother or sister

FRESCO: a painting made on a wall using wet plaster

GLYPH: a character or symbol meant to represent an idea or a sound

GUILD: a membership association of craftspeople or businesspeople

HAREM: the part of the palace reserved for women

HEIR: a person who inherits property or a title

HERESY: a belief that is very different from commonly held beliefs

HERETIC: someone whose beliefs (especially religious beliefs) are not in line with generally accepted beliefs

ILLUMINATED MANUSCRIPT: a handwritten manuscript decorated with illustrations in colored ink and gold leaf

IMPALE: to pierce through with a sharp object

LOOT: to take the goods of a population after a battle

MALIGN: to speak critically of

MORTUARY TEMPLE: a temple built to house the tomb of a pharaoh

OBELISK: a tall stone pillar

PAGAN: religion that originated before or outside of the world's main religions

PATRON SAINT: a (no longer living) holy person who protects a place

PLUNDER: to steal goods and destroy property

REGENT: someone who rules or administers for a monarch who is too young to rule

SACK: to destroy a town or village

SARCOPHAGUS: a stone coffin

SPOILS: goods that are forcibly taken or stolen

INDEX